Art Textiles of the World: Great Britain

TELOS

© Telos Art Publishing 1996

Edited by Matthew Koumis
Photography by James Johnson
Designed and Typeset by Celsius, Winchester
Printed by Weston Colour Ltd, Southampton

ISBN 0 9526267 2 1 (softback)
ISBN 0 9526267 7 2 (hardback)

A CIP catalogue record for this book is available from the British Library

Cover illustration:
Sally Greaves-Lord
Silk Scarves (1996)
Hand-painted on spun silk
74" x 16", 190 x 42cm
photo: FXP

Photo credits:
p13-22, 36, 37, 40 FXP; p23 Heidi Kosaniuk; p35 Tim Hill; p39, 41 Mark Pinder; p52-57 Max Alexander;
p54 Andreas Schmidt; p66 Len Grant, courtesy of Whitworth Art Gallery; p67 Peter White, courtesy of
Crafts Council; p69 David Bennett, courtesy of English Heritage/Northern Arts; p 72, 73, 77 John McKenzie;
p78 Mike Davidson; p79 David Ogden; p81 Antonia Reeve, courtesy of Scottish Office; p82, 83, 88 Dewi
Tannat Lloyd; p 102, 103, 105 courtesy of Christopher Farr; p111 (b&w portrait) Loise Bobbé.

Preface

This book is a celebration of the rich diversity of art textiles that have emanated from the British Isles in recent years. Focusing in depth on ten textile artists it explores the vibrant tapestries of Jo Barker and Marta Rogoyska; the elegantly minimalist tapestries of Sara Brennan and woven structures of Greg Parsons; the delicately stitched, quilted hangings of Lynn Setterington; the abstract, printed textiles of Kate Blee and Sally Greaves-Lord; and the more figurative work of Dawn Dupree, Jeanette Appleton and Nicola Henley.

The need to explore and take risks if ideas are to remain fresh is a constant challenge. What shines through in all the interviews is the artists' dedicated and determined approach to their work, in spite of many competing commitments and pressures. Quite apart from the wealth of illustrations, the profiles provide an insight into both individual and shared concerns, whether they are emphasising a passion for colour or uncompromising quality, or expanding on the importance of landscape, travel, other cultures or history.

Given the current paucity of publications generally available on contemporary textile arts this book, the first in a series devoted to world textiles, is a doubly welcome initiative.

Barley Roscoe MBE
Director of the Holburne Museum and Crafts Study Centre, Bath

Editor's Foreword

Textile art is coming of age. Its overwhelming combination of line, colour and texture makes it a powerful artform whose importance is at last being acknowledged by curators and collectors worldwide.

Art Textiles of the World is a new series celebrating some of the finest international talent. Volume One focuses on the exciting young generation of British textile artists working in printed and painted textile art and design, tapestry, embroidery, weave and felt. One hundred wide-ranging illustrations are illuminated by conversation with the artists, offering insights into their outlook on life, sources of inspiration, methods of working, choice of medium and recent commissions. An authoritative essay by Amanda Fielding, Curator of the Crafts Council Collection, explores some of the shared objectives raised by the artists.

I wish to thank the many people who have generously given advice during the conception of this series, including Janet de Boer of TAFTA; Diana Drummond of Buckinghamshire College; Tim Earnshaw; Edward Fennel of The Times; Amanda Fielding and Clare Buckle of the Crafts Council; Shelly Goldsmith and colleagues at Winchester School of Art; Dr Jennifer Harris of the Whitworth Art Gallery; David Herbert of The Herbert Press; Maureen Hodge and colleagues at Edinburgh College of Art; Melanie Miller and colleagues at Manchester Metropolitan University; Keiren Phelan at Southern Arts; Michael Spender of the Embroiderers' Guild; Dr Janet Summerton; and Audrey Walker MBE.

I would also like to thank Margie Barton, Humphrey Carr, David Hyde and Judith Maclean at Celsius, Penny Knollys, Adriana Lopez, Miranda McKearney, Sophie Pattinson, Clare Williams, and my wife for her unfailing patience. For kindly lending work to be photographed thanks are due to Mary LaTrobe Bateman of Contemporary Applied Arts, London; Denise Collins of CCA Galleries, Cambridge; and Amanda Game of the Scottish Gallery, Edinburgh. Quotations from Cézanne on page 11 are taken from 'Cézanne by Himself' published by Macdonald & Co.

Matthew Koumis

Introduction

To achieve their very individual goals, the ten artists featured in this book draw on one or more traditional textile techniques, including tapestry, embroidery, weaving, printing and felting. Each one of these processes has its established applications and set of standards, its own specific history, pioneers and landmarks, such as seminal exhibitions and innovatory training courses. Over the twentieth century they have all been adapted to express abstract and narrative ideas. Since the British 'Crafts Revival' of the early 1970s, rules have been broken in all the craft disciplines, from textiles to glass, ceramics to metalwork, furniture to jewellery, as individuals, benefiting from new art school training and improved professional opportunities, have experimented with materials and processes to create radical and challenging artefacts.

As art school graduates and postgraduates, those featured in this volume are imbued with the notion of fine art textiles and the sense of individual creativity. Attitudes towards process and its significance vary from one maker to the next. Marta Rogoyska is realistic about the gruelling and time-consuming aspects of tapestry weaving and flatly claims that she is not obsessed by technique. Nicola Henley on the other hand clearly enjoys the reflective nature of embroidery and finds the decision making involved in printing and painting very mentally stimulating. Sally Greaves-Lord admits that she 'wanted a discipline where the process and craft of it played a big part'. But whatever their differences of opinion about process, all these makers are united in the search for a personal aesthetic language.

The impact of fine art training and fine art is inescapable. Many makers describe the importance of looking and drawing before they embark on their textiles. Out in the wild landscape, Nicola Henley becomes very absorbed in the crucial activities of bird-watching and sketching in chalks, crayons and paint. Sara Brennan finds drawing a more intense phase compared to the relaxed activity of tapestry weaving. Time after time the names of certain painters crop up because their aesthetic – very likely modernist – has struck a particular chord. Kate Blee and Greg Parsons mention Mark Rothko as a powerful influence on their approaches to colour, while Jo Barker enthuses over Patrick Heron's colour palette and Sara Brennan acknowledges a debt to American abstract painters such as Agnes Martin and Robert Ryman. Ryman's large white canvases, his use of hundreds of whites, led Brennan to blend many shades of white, in linen or cotton. Both Barker and Brennan have created the illusion of painting in their tapestries – Barker suggesting spontaneously drawn marks and bold sweeps of brushed colour, Brennan introducing irregular edges, pencil lines and sections of bare canvas. In Marta

Rogoyska's work there are echoes of the joie de vivre found in Matisse's cut outs and parallels with the work of other fine artists. Dawn Dupree relates her enjoyment of contemporary paintings to the fact she is 'working in the same way, in my own medium'.

And of course it is not just contemporary European and American painting which makes its presence felt in so many of these textiles. Not unlike many 19th century designers before them, a handful of these practitioners choose to look further afield and explore the potential of other cultures. Nicola Henley highlights the influence of cave paintings and Italian frescoes, while Jeannette Appleton speaks eagerly of North American Indian mythology, Babylonian legend and ancient stones. Lynn Setterington has immersed herself in the kantha embroidery of Bangladesh, finding inspiration in its stitching patterns and imagery taken from daily life.

Beyond process and forays into other cultures and fine art movements lies the fascinating and at times very intense area of personal motivation and commitment. Sally Greaves-Lord understands the compulsive aspect of personal creativity only too well. 'My work totally absorbs me – it's not always pleasurable, it's essential'. Often a maker's energies are bound up with the urge to express traces of emotion and experience and their work can become a focus for personal growth. This is not true in every case however. Note the difference between Jeannette Appleton's experience of felt-making to explore internal ideas and Greg Parsons' practice of sourcing structural ideas from the external world of architecture to develop his designs. Familiar objects may appear in Dawn Dupree's printed textiles, but to her they read as metaphors, referring to her family and relationships. Sara Brennan regards her tapestry as a narrative to her life and is pursuing her own aesthetic language to express the emotional experience of landscape. Jeanette Appleton's work has captured her feelings towards possessions and personal space, and her experience of letting go part of motherhood.

Several makers here speak of their concern to evoke a response from their audience, to create a dialogue. Kate Blee talks of wanting people to feel they could 'fall into, eat, or pick up' the vibrant colour she creates. Jo Barker wants her colour combinations to provoke an emotional reaction. 'I like it when people gasp'. Nicola Henley, drawn to the freedom and movement of birds, sees her gannets and choughs as important lead-in points for the viewer. 'I want to make work that people can relate to'.

Today's important requirements of creative diversity and professionalism within the applied arts can be found in the careers of these individuals as they rise to challenges from the worlds of public art, architecture, interior design, fashion and industry. Sally Greaves-Lord's creative range is especially astonishing as she turns her hand to designs for textiles, architectural glass, floor coverings and murals. A recent commission was to design four sets of wool curtains and four rugs, hand tufted by the Edinburgh Tapestry Company, for Belsay Hall, Northumberland. Dawn Dupree and Lynn Setterington were also involved in this furnishing project, Dupree producing two cushions, Setterington a quilted hanging. Tapestry's long tradition of enhancing interior spaces is particularly appropriate to the austere architectural environment of the twentieth century. Marta Rogoyska has designed tapestries for many prestigious clients, often commissioned by the Public Art Development Trust, while younger Jo Barker has already secured a number of significant commissions in the private and public sectors. Consistently designing for major companies and producing her own studio pieces, Kate Blee's response to commercial opportunities in the world of fashion and interiors has been exemplary. She is not precious about her work. 'I like my work to be used in a variety of ways, sparking out in all directions'. Greg Parsons, who has recently shifted away from making exclusively one-offs towards designing commercially viable furnishing fabrics, anticipates a similar approach. 'I feel that I can apply myself to the different areas that are open to me...I can see my work fitting into different categories'.

The ten interviews in this book reveal many of the themes which run through the development of contemporary textiles. They include the impact of fine art training and fine art, the expression of narrative and abstract ideas, and the creative potential between the individual artist and the commercial world. These statements celebrate those inherent qualities of yarn or cloth which differentiate textiles from painting, clearly affirming why these artists have chosen textiles as their expressive medium.

Amanda Fielding
Curator and writer

The most seductive thing
about art is the personality
of the artist…

Painting, as with any art,
comprises a technique,
a workman-like handling of
material; but the accuracy of
a tone and the felicitous
combination of effects
depend entirely on the
choices made by the artist.

Paul Cézanne (1839–1906)

Dawn Dupree

I'm passionate about colour, about the effect it has on me. I'm also exploring the possibilities of expression in relationships, something which affects us all.

Ripe Fruit (1991)
Dyed, printed and painted cotton sateen
55" x 40", 140 x 102cm

Opposite: Jealousy (1995)
Dyed, printed and painted cotton satin
50" x 49", 197 x 125cm

My studio is my peace. I like it here. I've been here four years.

Back home we've got the sort of house where loads of people drop in. My partner's an artist too, so we're always fighting for time to work. I'm fighting for space in my head to keep inspired, not to get bogged down.

Some mornings I spend in a decompression chamber with my son Jody. He's six, he's got cerebral palsy. Later in the day one or two people come round to help us with his balance and coordination exercises, it used to be five hours a day – now we do an hour. Our other son Finlay is two. It's sort of sad about Jody; he can't walk, he has problems with his hands, but he's a great character, he's very bright and cocky, and like most kids he fights with his brother. I couldn't imagine life without children.

My mother used to tell me 'Don't stare!' But I do, I do. I watch other people's gestures and try and understand what's behind them. I get a real buzz when I feel I've captured the meaning behind a gesture. People say to me 'Your work is about fruit and figures and landscape, and you've travelled the world', and up to a point they're right. But there's more to it than that. I'm exploring the possibilities of expression in relationships, something which affects us all.

I'm passionate about colour, about the effect it has on me, and on the relationships between colours. A flower is never just a flower, it's a form which has its own colour and gesture, which sets up a relationship with another form and another colour in the same piece. The forms have developed: at first they were fruit, then they became more like animals or human figures. Now they're simplifying, I'm using circles and squares a lot.

On the one hand, I'm playing with my materials, I'm manipulating forms, colours and textures within a piece. On the other hand I'm revealing my own subconscious, it's about interconnecting moments of my past and present. Some moments are happy and exhilarating; others sad, even devastating.

Looking back on pieces like **Orange Figure** or **Yellow Figure**, it's funny to see shapes that remind me of flowers, or ice lollies, or balloons I blew up for Jody – totally trivial and unintentional things. Like a humorous celebration of life, but with a deeper undertone. Other pieces seemed much heavier at the time I made them, like Survival of the Fittest. This grew out of the story of this smallholding my mum and dad had. She recently split up from my dad. It was the end of an era. All the animals had to go.

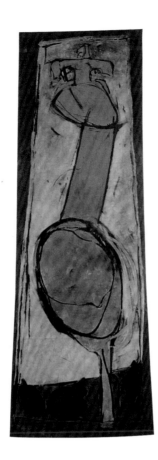

Left: Incubation (1994)
Dyed, printed and painted cotton satin
147" x 37", 374 x 94cm

Right: Germination (1994)
Dyed, printed and painted cotton satin
142" x 34", 371 x 87cm

I was recently involved in an exhibition at the Canterbury Museum and Art Gallery where I saw this huge painting of a cow. I assumed it would be called something like 'Cow in Landscape'. I thought it was brilliant. Then I read the title, it made me laugh out loud: 'Separated or Divorced'. It reminded me of **Retribution**. But not all my titles are heavy. I don't consider myself a sad person.

My mum is a cook. I was brought up in a pub. When I was a child, we moved around a lot, never lived anywhere for more than three years. I left home when I was sixteen and worked as a waitress. At seventeen I went to Beirut, the Middle East, North Africa. When I was nineteen I went right around the world, on my own. Looking back I'm amazed nothing awful happened to me. If I had a seventeen year old daughter who wanted to travel to Beirut, I'm sorry but I'd say no!

I got kicked out of my first foundation course, because I never turned up. At Southwark College I did my foundation year and finally started taking it seriously. I didn't get in to Goldsmiths' first time round, so I went to Spain for a year, applied again and got in. Over the three years of the course, I considered Spain my home and lived a kind of double life over there.

16

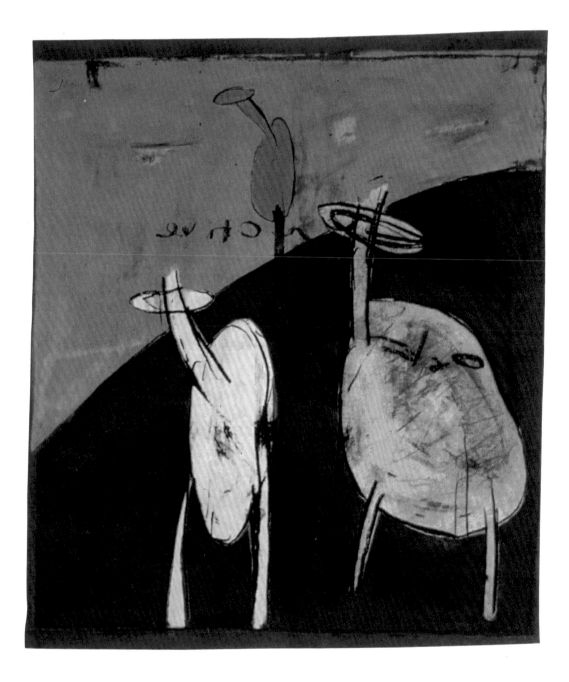

Instinctive Behaviour (1995)
Dyed, printed and painted cotton satin
48" x 47", 122 x 120cm

I'd been writing some notes in my sketchbook which bled through to the preparatory drawings – I thought it would be an interesting experiment to follow this through on an actual piece.

Retribution (1996)
Dyed, printed and painted cotton satin
97" x 59", 247 x 18cm

Goldsmiths' was great. Everyone seemed more knowledgeable than me, I found that really hard, a total trauma to work surrounded by some really brilliant people. Goldsmiths' got rid of all the emotional shit in my life – dreams and so on – it all came out, and when I came out the other end it was like the beginning of my artistic life. I had the tools, the knowledge, and the most essential ingredient was how to work on my own.

At one point I decided to become a painter, but my tutor said she felt I got a lot of fulfilment out of the controlled side of printing. It's true that a lot of the techniques I use do involve planning and preparation. Enlarging the drawing, coating the screen, dyeing the cloth, it takes days. Even just getting the screens ready involves blasting off the old image, coating it, exposing it under UV light. The actual making, the printing and painting, doesn't take so long, but it's much harder because I'm making aesthetic and practical decisions about the way colours might go. Even though at times it's a bit of a frustrating technique, I do find it really exciting. I don't use weighing scales – I just guess everything. I like working like that, it's what I'm like as a person. When I see a splodge I might work into it. If I've made a mistake, spilled something onto it, if some ink comes off the edge of the screen, it's never a disaster.

Sometimes my techniques change by accident. It's only when I look back I realise that they're altering. I like to play around with the pigments, it's like a process of adding and taking away. I used to start off with a vague idea in my mind of what I wanted to do, and make a group of drawings or paintings on a certain idea; but now over the last year I've changed my way of working, it's less planned, it's become totally spontaneous.

Orange Figure for example has some painterly areas that I wanted to look really spontaneous, so I had to keep redoing it. I wanted it to be done in one movement, I had to do it about six times in all. When the piece comes out of the steamer, the things that come out and I say 'Oh no!' often turn out to be the best pieces.

I do get tired of printing in the studio sometimes. It's very divorced from the thinking side of it, and from the exhibiting side. A lot of people don't see that. Students sometimes ring up and want to come and see me, and they're a bit surprised to see how unglamorous studio life is.

In general I relate to painting best: I'm working in the same way, in my own medium. I prefer minimal or abstract work, and work that's not similar to mine. I like De Kooning's abstract figurative painting, it's got a very physical energy. I like the texture in Paul Klee, and his drawn line. I like the depth and richness of colour in Patrick Heron's work. In textiles I like Sally Greaves-Lord's colour.

I'm depressed when I haven't got anything in my mind or on the go. I've got to be involved. It's not important whether it's for a show or not. I've never had time to promote my work – I just make it, that's all I've got time to do. I'm lucky that I've had to concentrate just on making my work. I think it's helped me develop my ideas without too much sidetracking. I would like to work on a really large scale because I've had shows in galleries where I'm a bit restricted by space – my hangings work better on a large scale.

I never seriously think of giving up. My work is my life.

Protecting the Elements (1993)
Dyed, printed and painted cotton satin
66" x 46", 169 x 117cm

Isolation (1996)
Dyed, printed and painted cotton satin
73" x 48", 187 x 122cm

Dawn Dupree

Born

1964, London

Education and Awards

1983–85 – Southwark College of Art, Diploma in Art and Design

1986–89 – Goldsmiths' College, London, BA (Hons) Fine Art/Textiles

1987 – Inter-London Art Colleges Competition, First Prize

1991 – Crafts Council Setting Up Grant

Orange Figure (1996)

Dyed, printed and painted cotton satin

72" x 59", 184 x 127cm

Selected Exhibitions

1991 – Two Women Show, Omphalus Gallery, London

1992 – New Fibre Art with California Fibres Group Show, USA

1993 – New Faces, Crafts Council Shop, V & A Museum, London

1994 – Works for 94, Crafts Council Gallery, London

1994 – Colour into Cloth, Crafts Council Gallery, London

1994 – Society of Designer Craftsmen, Mall Galleries, London

1994–95 – Touring Showcase, Eastern Arts, Lincolnshire

1996 – Hardly a Stitch, Royal Museum and Art Gallery, Canterbury

1996 – Group Show, Marks & Spencer Headquarters, London

1996 – Summer Show, Contemporary Applied Arts

1997 – Two Women Show, Walford Mill, Dorset

1997 – Levis Gallery, London (solo)

1997 – Showcase, Horniman Museum, London

Public Commissions

1988 – Fashion design drawings for 'Blue Mondays', San Diego, California

1996 – Living at Belsay

On-going commissions for furnishing fabrics and wall-hangings

Collections

Crafts Council of Great Britain

**My work is like a celebration of life,
but with a deeper undertone**

Yellow Figure (1996)
Dyed printed and painted cotton drill
72" x 50", 184 x 127cm

Sara Brennan

**I remember one day going up a hill, it might have been snowing. I was on horseback. We were beside a fence – a line of posts and wires. The mist was coming down, everything was so quiet yet so vast.
That's what it's all about.**

Green Bands I, II, III, IV (1995)
Woven tapestries
40" x 40", 96 x 96cm each

Opposite: Broken Grey Line I (1994)
Woven tapestry
42" x 36", 106 x 92cm

I remember one day going up a hill, it might have been snowing. I was on horseback. We were beside a fence – a line of posts and wires. The mist was coming down, everything was so quiet yet so vast. That's what its all about.

Horse-riding is the easiest form of hill-walking, with the added bonus of being on an animal. It's so far removed from the studio, yet it's got so much to do with everything. A gut, honest thing that you get. I once galloped in the dark (by mistake!).

There's an austerity and a very educated politeness here in Edinburgh, a strict Protestant work ethic. Everything is very understated. Sometimes it's really frustrating, you get tied in knots. It comes over in my work, I put a restraint on it. I'm a very messy person, but I try to keep my studio very tidy. I'm clinging on to being organised, but it's a real battle.

My work is a narrative to my life. It's quite autobiographical. I've moved around a fair bit. I don't know whether art sublimates my emotions but it certainly adds to my problems!

When I left school I went to Papua New Guinea for a year at the National Arts School – it was wonderful, I had an amazing time. I went on to Edinburgh College of Art, thinking I was going to be a painter or a sculptor. I did a first year general course, like a foundation year, moving on to the BA in Tapestry, still at Edinburgh.

Deer 1 (1987)
Woven tapestry
24" x 50", 61 x 130cm

Rocket I (1989)
Woven tapestry
10" x 8", 25 x 19cm

In 1989 I was awarded a Scottish Arts Council residency at Nobel's Explosives Company. Rather ironically the Peace Prize is named after the same man. The site was massive: there were deer and herons, factories and offices, everything surrounded by a twenty-mile perimeter fence. **Rocket I** is a slightly cynical piece showing one of the old Victorian buildings shooting off like a rocket, leaving a sterile stump which represents the arid financial systems and dubious ethics of the place.

Anyway on the whole the residency was great. I did it with a sculptor. We got paid to concentrate on our work. Most days and nights we were working and talking about the work, it was a completely surreal experience. Afterwards I moved to Aberdeenshire, but it didn't work out, partly because it was so cold! And I became a bit mad living out there in a rural remote area.

For me the work from that period was significant in terms of what it led to. I had something to aim for, as my friend Jo Barker had organised a show for Aberdeen Art Gallery, who invested heavily in the pair of us – a big gallery space with a colour catalogue. It was a key show for both of us, a leap ahead from the libraries and cafés we'd shown in until then. Afterwards I moved back to Edinburgh. Things changed. I got the studio and got on with it. I got my life sorted out. I lost the romance to a certain extent. Things became less furious. It all started to distil.

My work is evocative of landscape. You can either take it literally as being about fields, such as corn fields, or else in the abstract as zones or fields of colour. I'm interested in natural lines, controlled lines. A line of trees on the horizon has the appearance of a natural landscape, but at some stage they've been manipulated. That's what I'm exploring in **Green Bands I-IV**.

The evocation of fields – the rich texture of a ploughed field, also affects the surface. The surface you get from weaving you don't get anywhere else. It's rich, it's tactile, it's got depth. It's not a thin layer, it's dense. Materials are crucial – it's to do with what can happen by placing yarns. There's enough happening if you get it right to make the piece sing. The reaction that's caused, the atmosphere that's caused is enough.

I'd been using old yarn – but there are certain tones you can't get anymore such as the olive/mustard in the Vertical Field series. Recently, with a grant from the Scottish Arts Council, I've been able to invest into getting my own yarn dyed up. But it's a very tricky process, and I'm very particular: there's a piece I've had to unpick three times now as I'm still not satisfied the tone is right.

My work has vertical and horizontal blocks, lines and areas. This can be traced back through all my work, and has become more refined. There is also a consistent colour palette, using one or two predominant colours. My recent works are more hard edged, they're removed. There's a slight twist to some of the lines, a hidden line of red or yellow giving a subtle definition. As with all tapestry, they have a softness and a tactile quality. They're evocative – it doesn't stop there.

I prefer working in a series, creating a body of work. This relates to the nature of tapestry – it takes so long to weave something, it's good to feel you don't always have to go back to square one and research an embryonic idea, but that there can be some continuity in treating a subject.

I like the work of 1950s American minimalists: the big white canvases of Robert Ryman; the sculptures of Donald Judd; the ethereal canvases of Agnes Martin. Her work is spatial and intimate (an unusual combination), they're very plain, within them there's a quietness. Among Renaissance painters I admire Masaccio for his simplicity and for the sculptural depth of his drawing.

I dream that one day I'll be able to write a thesis about something quite unrelated to textiles, such as archeology. For example, to take a rural area four miles square, and research its land use, social and economical.

What brings me back to tapestry over and over again is that it has a real presence. It glows. It is scarce. It's relatively uncharted territory as a contemporary art form. I went to Sydney with my dad, and every third building we saw we would say – 'My God, there's a tapestry'. Here in Britain, if we're lucky, there's one or two pieces chosen to keep the Director's wife happy.

Ploughed Field Black Hill and Cloud (1991)
Woven tapestry
19" x 17", 49 x 42cm

Black and Yellow Field with Whites (1993)
Woven tapestry
56" x 48", 142 x 122cm

To be a tapestry weaver it helps if you're a tactile person. But there's a risk with tapestry, that people get carried away with the making. It becomes a way of life, and then everyone's too cautious to criticise. Constructive criticism is very absent.

I'd be very interested in a show devoted to a small group of tapestry artists, such as William Jefferies – he's doing something three-dimensional that's not been done before. I also like Clio Padovani, she's pushing it, and not stopping at the weaving side of it.

I've only sold three large tapestries in my life. But if I had to make money from my work, I'd do another job which offered a ready-made career structure, rather than compromise my work weaving drinks coasters. I work at the Museum of Modern Art in the café three or four days a week. It's very exhausting, but it does give me a sense of security – I've worked there on and off for ten years now.

This is it, this is my home, this is my life. I'm happy. I've got a lovely partner, a nice house, I teach an evening class at the art college. I'm in contact with other artists. It becomes a way of life, time now to focus in on the work.

Art Textiles of the World: Great Britain

Above: Vertical Field III (1995)
Opposite: Vertical Field/Thin Line I (1995)
Woven tapestries
8" x 8", 20 x 20cm

There's a slight twist to some of the lines, together with a hidden line of red or yellow; there's just enough happening to make the piece evocative, to make it sing.

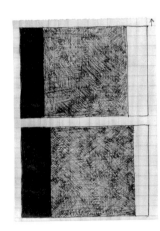
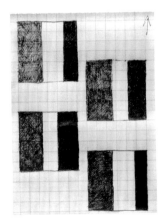

Sketch (1996)

Sara Brennan

Born

1963, Edinburgh

Education and Awards

1981–82 – National Arts School, Papua New Guinea

1982–86 – Edinburgh College of Art, BA (Hons) Tapestry

1989 – Scottish Arts Council/ICI, Artist in Residence

1991 – Scottish Arts Council/Highland Regional Council, Artist in Residence

1993 – Hope-Scott Trust Award for 'Works for 94' Exhibition

1995 – Scottish Arts Council, Artistic Development Award

Selected Exhibitions

1992 – Fine Art Consultancy, Shad Thames Gallery, London

1993 – Interwoven II, The Smith's Galleries, London

1993 – The Collective Gallery, Edinburgh

1994 – Works for '94, Crafts Council

1994 – New Art in Scotland, CCA, Glasgow, Aberdeen Art

1994 – Images of the Earth, Fruitmarket Gallery, Edinburgh and
    Sotheby's, London

1995 – British Tapestry Exhibition, The Harley Gallery, Notts

1995 – Raw Materials, Contemporary Scottish Textiles (tour)

1995 – Sara Brennan & Louise Hopkins' Project Room, Collective

1996 – Woven Image, Contemporary British Tapestry, Barbican Centre (tour)

1996 – Group Show, Karsten Schubert Gallery, London

Collections

Aberdeen City Art Gallery and Museums

Two Fields – Black Vertical (1996)
Woven tapestry
8" x 8", 20 x 20cm

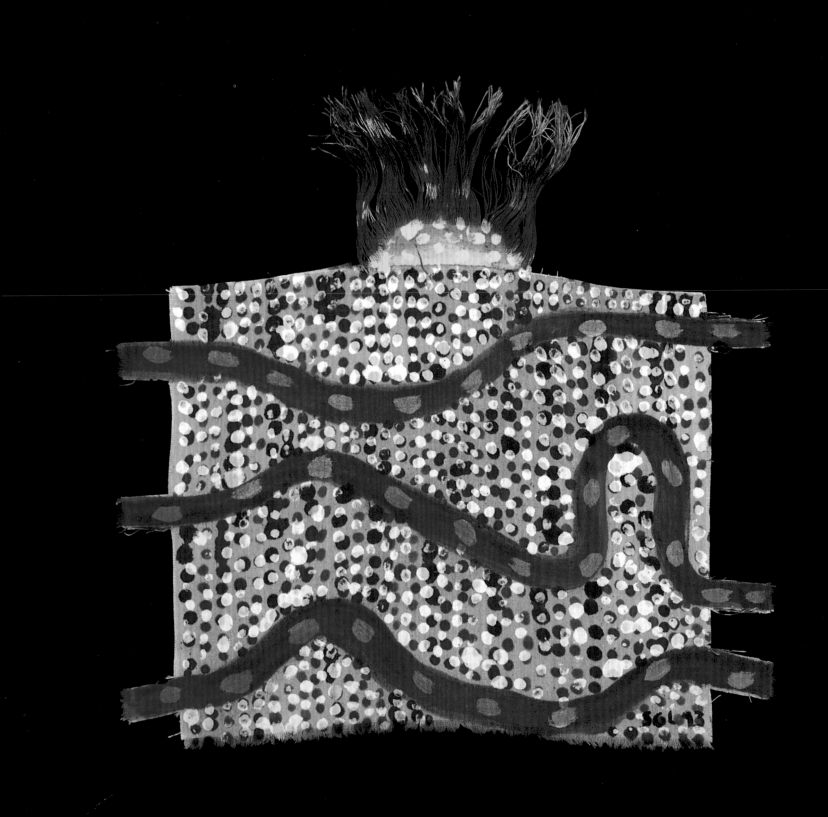

Sally Greaves-Lord

In all my work I try to keep the shapes I use simple, universal. Each element can be seen from different viewpoints: things approaching whole things and then breaking them up, maybe destroying them, maybe not.

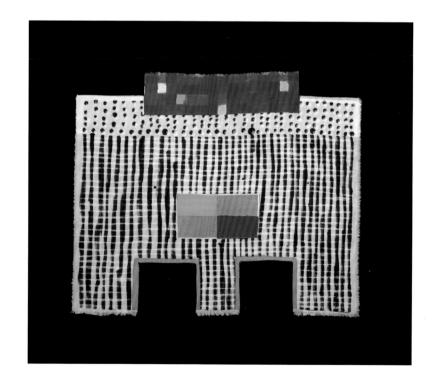

Little Building (1992)
Hand-painted on spun silk
13" x 10", 33 x 27cm
(Commissioned for Issey Miyake)

Opposite: Spotted Piece (1993)
Hand-painted on silk noil poplin
9" x 8", 22 x 21cm
(Commissioned for Issey Miyake)

I still remember the private view of my exhibition at Contemporary Applied Arts in 1988. It was the last time I had a really short hair cut. A certain phase of my life had ended. Tessa Peters and Tatjana Marsden hung the work beautifully. I sold all the collection, except one piece which I've kept. They were bought by the V & A; the Holburne Museum and Craft Study Centre, Bath; the Contemporary Art Society; and various private collectors. I was absolutely thrilled. I wanted them to be wanted.

The show came at a good time, six years after I'd left the Royal College of Art. For a few years I'd been making a series of smaller pieces, often selling them as designs – I was dying to do a large scale piece. I rented a huge print table at Clockwork Studios in Brixton for the twelve months leading up to the show. The banners are painted on spun silk. I've never liked working on complicated weaves, I prefer very flat cloth. It was understated, minimal, it almost looked like cotton but felt like silk. The composition, not the colour, was primary for me. I didn't want anything to detract from it. I love cloth. I feel passionate about it. These pieces were quite monumental and striking in what they communicated.

I was ready to leave London. I was immersed in my work to the exclusion of everything else. I used to feel guilty about doing anything else: there wasn't anything I wanted to do other than work. For the nine years I'd lived there after college, I'd rarely left the city at weekends, I'd worked nearly all the time. I had the feeling that, once the exhibition of the banners was over, I could move on.

So one Friday I packed my car with as many of my things as I could possibly squeeze in. I gave up the London flat which I had been renting, and came to live in this 18th Century dyer's cottage in Yorkshire which I had bought a year earlier. I had been coming up to Yorkshire on holiday since I was eight, it was always a very magical place. In London, try as I might, I simply couldn't find any feeling for colour. I had always used pencil, black ink and black paint. In Yorkshire that changed. Living close to the sea and to the great mass of the moors has undoubtedly fed my work.

I'm now doing a much wider variety of work for many different clients. In addition to textiles I design sculptures, murals, stationery and glass. This range of work is not without its dangers. But on the whole it feels healthy for my work to take new forms. And for my creative work to progress fundamentally, it's always textiles that I turn to.

Banner (1988)
Hand-painted on spun silk
195" x 36", 500 x 92cm

At the moment I'm making a series of scarves. I keep to a strict routine. I get up at 7.30am and I'll do some work straight away. Then I'll shower and breakfast. When I'm engrossed in my work, time is irrelevant to me. I have to remind myself to eat. There's no separation between me and the work. If a friend rings and asks me to go for a walk I say no. My work is absolutely compulsive. It totally absorbs me. It's not always pleasurable, it's essential. I've got all the shapes, patterns, textures in mind. I can feel the relationship of one to another.

Getting the work out of the steamer is a very thrilling moment. I unroll the backing cloth out in the yard, usually four scarves at a time. The dyes really smell. Once they're steamed, the colours change – nowadays I have quite a good idea of how they'll look. Then I wash them off, a laboured process, and when they're almost dry I iron them. It's often midnight by now. I hold them up in front of the mirror. Finally I like to roll the edges myself if I have time. The whole process is very sensual, the cloth, the colours, the tactile quality of it all.

I haven't trained as a painter. I felt from the beginning that I wanted a discipline where the process and craft played a big part. In all my work I try to keep the shapes I use simple, universal. Each element can be seen from different viewpoints: things approaching whole things and then breaking them up, maybe destroying them, maybe not. Some things stand solid and unbreakable, while other things are whizzing round them.

In a series of hangings which I made in June 1996 for the Brewery Arts Centre, Kendall, I gave my work titles for the first time: Day Time; Mourning; **Even**, Sun Set. The titles reflect the flexibility of the pieces, encompassing both the inner and outer landscape.

Looking back to past projects, one that was particularly important to me was the new design for the Issey Miyake shop in Sloane Street. As a result Issey Miyake invited me to work as their creative director in the UK, which I did freelance for five years. It was a brilliant job. I did some work with the Japanese side of the company, but mostly I worked with the London shops, creating their window installations and their overall look. I developed my role to include borrowing or commissioning work from various artists and designers. Matthew Marchbank made a most wonderful beechwood forest for a Christmas window. It was an amazing opportunity because it brought me in contact with lots of other artists and designers. I'd only done my own work until then, now I had to design and make things which complemented other peoples' work as well as having intrinsic value.

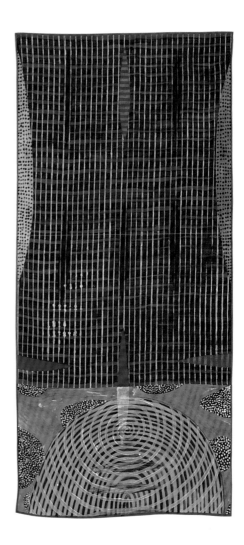

Even (1996)
Hand-painted on spun silk
59" x 36", 200 x 92cm

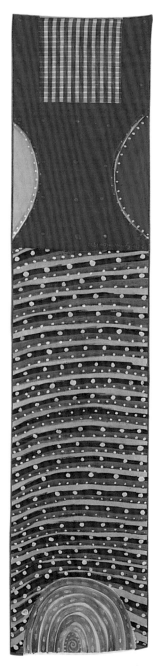

My work is absolutely compulsive. It totally absorbs me. I've got all the shapes, patterns, textures in mind. I can feel the relationship of one to another.

Silk Scarves (1996)
Hand-painted on spun silk
74" x 16", 190 x 42cm

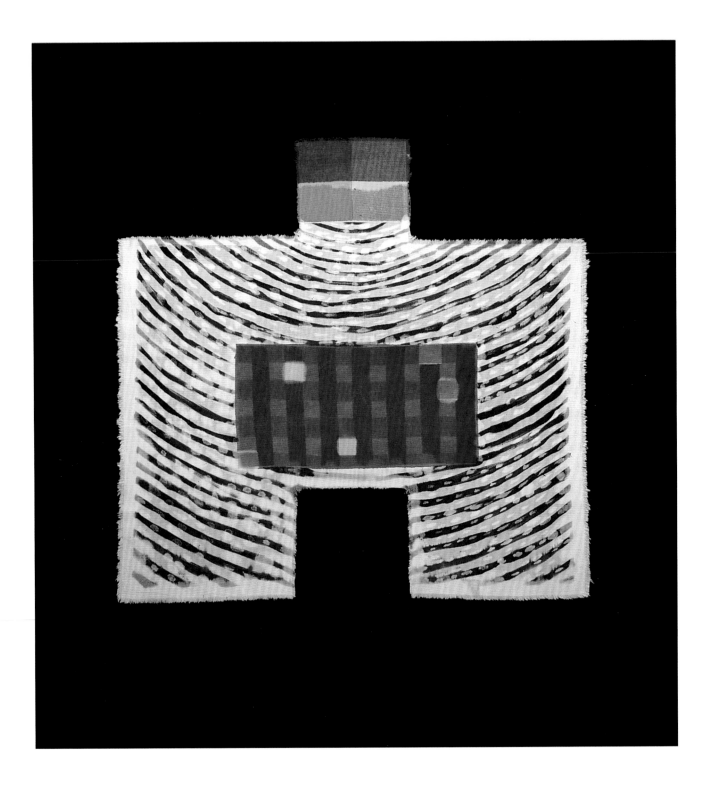

Little Building (1992)
Hand-painted on spun silk
13" x 12", 31 x 33cm
(Commissioned for Issey Miyake)

Ochre Belsay Rug (1996)
Hand gun-tufted in pure wool
118" x 88", 300 x 225cm
(Commissioned for Living at Belsay, made by
the Edinburgh Tapestry Company)

Spotted Piece and **Little Buildings** emerged from a series of designs that I did for Issey Miyake. They were a very flexible organisation to work for – they'd give me only a tiny swatch of colours which were going in the next collection, and then only if I asked for it. These pieces are more organic, flowing, watery. I'm particularly fond of them.

A project I've recently worked on is called 'Living at Belsay'. Belsay Hall is an English Heritage property in Northumberland. The work involved the refurnishing of five of its rooms in a contemporary style. All the work commissioned will be auctioned. Northumberland County Council commissioned four rugs and four curtains from me, and asked me to collaborate with the Edinburgh Tapestry Company who would make the rugs. They bring to their gun tufted rugs the same integrity with which they have been creating their exquisite tapestries for the last century. With each rug we would sit down together and they would do a tufted sample (which looks like a shaving brush) of each area of the rug. Literally translating the painted design into yarn simply doesn't work – it's more a question of interpretation, of understanding how the colour and texture of yarns work.

As a student at Farnham I was painfully aware how unworldly I was. I do find life intensely difficult and I must admit to having felt the occasional pang of envy for those who seem to breeze through. As a child I had a recurring dream of threads getting all tangled up... I can only work effectively when I'm alone. When I'm making a piece I go through times of awful doubt. But I encourage myself to trust that it does come right in the end, if not without great struggle. It's a bit like Pandora's box – once it's open, there's no closing it.

Sally Greaves-Lord

Born

1957, Sutton Coldfield

Education and Awards

1976–77 – Bourneville School of Arts and Crafts

1977–80 – West Surrey College of Art and Design, BA (Hons)
Woven and Printed Textiles (First Class)

1980–82 – Royal College of Art, MA Textiles

1983 – Crafts Council Setting up Grant

1984 – Crafts Council Exhibition Grant

1992 – Art for Architecture, Civic Centre Project, Southampton

Selected Exhibitions

1994 – Colour into Cloth at the Crafts Council

1994 – Whitworth Art Gallery, Manchester

1994 – Holburne Museum and Crafts Study Centre, Bath

1996 – Contemporary Applied Art, London

1996 – Fibre Art, Brewery Arts Centre, Kendal

1996 – Egg, Knightsbridge (solo)

Selected Commissions and Consultancies

1979–83 – Timney Fowler, Printed Textile Design

1986 – Virgin Records, painted interior of roof garden

1989 – BBC, painted mural for television programme

1985–1991 – Issey Miyake International Ltd, Creative Director

1991 – Issey Miyake UK Ltd, design work

1992 – Southampton Civic Centre, design of glass screen and mural

1993–94 – Display designs for Silhouette Spectacles

1996 – Living at Belsay (in collaboration with Edinburgh Tapestry Company)

1996 – Painted shelter for Respite Centre, Oxfordshire (with John Hobson)

Collections

V & A Museum, London

Crafts Council of Great Britain

BUPA, London

Arthur Anderson, London

Long Term Credit Bank of Japan, London

Museum of Modern Art, Kyoto

Issey Miyake window installation, London (1989)
Papier mâché disc, distressed, painted in acrylics
78", 200cm diameter

Opposite: Blue Belsay Rug (1996)
Hand gun-tufted in pure wool
118" x 88", 300 x 225cm
(Commissioned for Living at Belsay)

Nicola Henley

Opposite: Plover Movements II (detail) (1995)
Silk-screen printed, painted and embroidered
15" x 65", 39 x 165cm

Coal-tits (detail) (1986)
43" x 56"; 110 x 143cm

I want to capture the contrast between intricate ornithological detail and vast expanses of space.

Portraying birds is a way of drawing people into the work. It gives the viewer a real intimacy. Often at private views people will talk to me about birds before they'll talk about art – the composition, the texture – the sides I'm maybe more interested in. But the birds are the lead-in point for people. I want to make work that people can relate to. Sometimes I'm wary of doing something overtly decorative, but from time to time I loosen up: I might add more decorative elements like stars on a flag for example. Stars and ravens are a combination I enjoy – one so black and earthy, the other so bright and infinite.

Since I came to Ireland from England five years ago, I've been influenced by the landscape and the colours of the sombre, moody skies and mountains. The textures in my work have become subtler too; the work has become more reflective. In earlier years I was concerned with mastering the technical skills. But now I've got time to concentrate on the composition, to think about pushing myself artistically.

Every piece comes from drawings in my sketch book. I use chalks, pencil crayons, water crayons, paint, and sometimes gold water-based paint. Sometimes I get involved in drawing the birds more analytically, to understand their form and movement. Fundamentally what appeals to me is their freedom of movement. You can draw rabbits or cows, but birds are the only things that have complete freedom to move in three dimensions, other than fish. I've thought about working with fish, I've sometimes drawn them. But fish are captured in water, as a confining element, while with birds the expanse of air above draws you up.

Gull Movements, Fanore (1996)
Silk-screen printed and painted on dyed calico; collaged with
paper and muslin. Machine and hand-embroidery
33" x 56", 97 x 143cm

**In Gull Movements, Fanore I wanted
to capture the quintessential
essence of the bird and how it
relates to the air currents around it,
and to the movement of the sea.
The orange represents a bolt of
movement, lightning in the dark.**

Stars and ravens are a combination I enjoy – one so black and earthy, the other so bright and infinite.

Ravens, Coolawn (1995)
Silk-screen printed, painted and embroidered
57" x 74", 144 x 213cm

Most of the images or marks are screen printed. The backgrounds are sometimes partly painted-in from the back of the cloth – it bleeds through giving a sense of three-dimensional space. I paint on the front as well to get a depth of shading. On some of my more recent pieces the borders have become part of the design, they contain the movement. I didn't want to close it in before – now I like the idea of working within a page, as if it were in a sketch book.

I wouldn't be happy just printing the piece – the embroidery is essential in expressing the textile quality of the work. If not I may as well be a painter, or a printer, but I'm not working on paper – I'm working on fabric, and I want the viewer to be very aware of that. I enjoy being able to express my ideas in fabric and stitch.

It might take me two days to prepare the drawings, the material, the screens. When I start printing I can print for three to four days. Once I've printed the main piece I put it up on the wall; I screen-print images on materials such as muslin, silk and paper. I can then select from this collection of printed material and paper, rather like using a painter's palette. After pinning them on and standing back to assess, I'll spend some time positioning and repositioning the pieces until I'm satisfied. They're then collaged onto the background using embroidery.

The embroidery I do is primarily machine embroidery, on an old fashioned 1950s Jones machine. The hand stitching is fairly minimal. I enjoy the process – it's more reflective, more tempered than printing. When I'm printing or painting I feel very much on edge – every mark feels crucial. I'm trying to predict the effect of every stroke, every mark, every print that I make. When I'm embroidering I feel more peaceful.

I often use the stitching behind the bird, like the memory of passing through time in a sequence. I also use it to draw the eye in when you're close. The print offers the scale and impact from a distance; but when you get close, it's the embroidery that keeps the textural interest. That's the reason I work from birds – they offer contrast between intricate detail and vast expanses of space. And collage helps to represent movement through time because I can use a build-up of layers to give hints of images which came before.

It's a whole process – you have an idea and you have to work through various stages to present the image. I'm building myself up psychologically when I'm going through those processes – I'm thinking about how I'm going to make them work together. I'm meditating through the process.

Cuckoo (1988)
Silk-screen printed, painted and embroidered
33" x 48", 83 x 123cm
(Collection of Galerie Pousse, Tokyo)

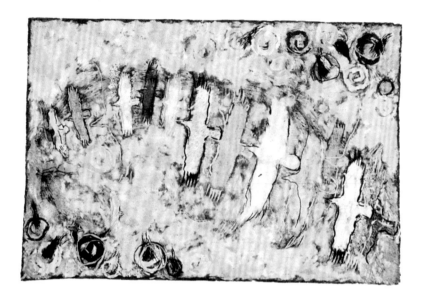

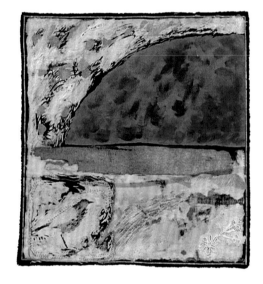

Top: Vultures (1990)
Silk-screen printed, painted and embroidered
33" x 48", 83 x 123cm

Waiting for Spring (1992)
Silk-screen printed, painted and embroidered
19" x 17", 49 x 45cm

Some pieces are intended simply to be studies of birds from the sketch books. Other pieces reflect my mood and are more personal to me.

My mother and brother were good ornithologists, as well as my husband Blair, so I've grown up fairly familiar with birds. Gradually I've got to know quite a lot of other people who are also inspired by birds and the natural environment such as Tim Johnson, Greg Poole and Kim Atkinson.

I've travelled throughout much of the world. In Nepal and India I was very taken with the architecture and colours of the stone, while **Vultures** was made after a trip to the Gambia, placing myself in the position of the birds above, imagining their view from the air of the village huts down below. Other influences include pre-Renaissance frescoes: I spent six months in Florence before I went on to art school. The process of bonding the colour with the plaster is similar to the way the discharge bonds with the cloth. With cave-paintings, which I saw in France, the ageing process is appealing.

When I was a student at Goldsmiths', I felt almost unbearably claustrophobic living in London. I would go to the top of buildings – St Paul's, Greenwich Observatory – with my sketch books, and draw aerial views as if I were a bird – a bird's eye perspective flying over the city, with abstract marks to represent this feeling of moving through the air. I felt a real thirst to escape the city.

I can't imagine moving back to England now – there's so much more space and freedom here. We've got three children, Max, 12, Erin, 9, and Georgia, 3, and it's a wonderful environment to bring them up in. Of course it's a struggle working with a young family. With Georgia I decided not to have a minder like I did with the older two – the early years pass so quickly, I wanted to be there for her, so from the beginning I brought her into the studio. But I have to admit now she's more disruptive I'm having second thoughts!

I do have a tendency to be over-reflective. But I have a stronger drive to maintain a zest for life, and that's what my work is about.

Sketchbook
Chalk on paper

50

Nicola Henley

Born

1960, Bristol

Education and Awards

1980–81 – Bristol Polytechnic, Foundation Course in Art
1981–84 – Goldsmiths' College, London, BA (Hons)
Embroidery/Textiles (First Class)
1986 – Crafts Council Setting-Up grant
1988 – South West Arts Project Award
1990 – British Council Travel Award, Japan
1994 – Leader Grant, East Clare Region, Ireland

Selected Exhibitions

1989 – Contemporary Applied Arts, London (solo)
1990 – Galerie Pousse, Tokyo (solo)
1991 – Christie's Annual Craft Auction, London
1992 – Out of the Frame, Crafts Council Gallery, London (tour)
1992 – Galerie Pousse, Tokyo (solo)
1994 – Contemporary Applied Arts, London
1993 – Visions of Craft, Crafts Council Gallery
1994 – Crafts Council Shop, V & A Museum
1995 – Organic Surfaces Crafts Council of Ireland, Dublin
1995 – Scottish Gallery, Edinburgh
1996 – Craftworks, Belfast
1996 – Oxford Gallery

Public Commissions

1985 – Greater London Council
1989 – John Radcliffe Hospital, Oxford

Collections

British Rail, St Pancras, London
Crafts Council of Great Britain
Embroiderers' Guild, London
Museum of Modern Art, Kyoto

Gannet's Plunge (1995)

Silk-screen printed, painted and embroidered

42" x 44", 112 x 107cm

Opposite: detail

Marta Rogoyska

My work is evocative of relationships. I'm fascinated by them. I'm a direct, uncomplicated person, and I operate in a simple, reactive way to people and to situations. My imagery is optimistic: it is zestful, dynamic, and full of joie de vivre.

Above left: Beach Sequence (1994)
Right: A Different Kind of Blue (1994)
Woven tapestries
45" x 45", 127 x 127cm each

Opposite: Thinking Aloud in Blue (1990)
Woven tapestry
74" x 88", 200 x 250cm

54

Triptych (1995)
Woven tapestry
215" x 50", 525 x 125cm each
(Commissioned for Glaxo Headquarters, UK)

Woven Tapestry (1988)
102" x 175", 270 x 450cm
(Commissioned for British Medical Association)

Sun Oil Triptych (detail) (1990)
Woven tapestry
189" x 78", 475 x 200cm
(Collection of Hunterian Museum, Glasgow)

Olivia, one of my twins, had done a painting at school and when I asked her what it was about she got quite upset. 'It's not a story, mummy, it's just a picture to look at!' I thought that was very profound. I usually tell people my work is evocative of relationships. I'm fascinated by them. I'm a direct, uncomplicated person, and I operate in a simple, reactive way to people and to situations. My imagery is optimistic: it is zestful, dynamic, and full of joie de vivre.

I listen to music a lot while I work: jazz piano in particular, people like Keith Jarrett. There's definitely an affinity between the abstract, improvisational fabric of music and my work. If you like, these are spontaneous jazz improvisations in collage or tapestry. I want my work to look as though it can always be rearranged. It's an interesting contradiction, since the making is so slow and pedantic. When asked to evoke a specific mood for a commission, I sometimes start by searching for a key: it could be a concept such as 'theatre', 'garden', 'window'. And then off I set, exploring a theme. It's quite funny that my work is ostensibly all those funny shapes and blobs and squints and squiggles. Yet every one I've agonised over! Every one is necessary to create that atmosphere.

Since the late 70s I've been doing collage out of frustration and necessity – liking a bit of this idea and wanting to retain a bit of that. Working with bits of torn, cut and found paper, being able to move it all around freely suited me very well. Partly because it is so insouciant, throw-away, a frozen moment in time.

The range of what I find stimulating to look at is very broad. In recent years I'm more and more drawn to landscape and topography. Being a Londoner, the discovery of nature in the raw absolutely blew me away. In Germany we lived in a beautiful tiny village perched on the top of a mountain, overlooking a massive forest. The dramatic changes that occurred with the changing seasons knocked me out with their force, vitality and inevitability. Here in California the desert, the light, the flora and fauna are awe-inspiring. And recently discovering the tropics in their abundance – the whole experience has completely altered my perceptions, and has actually made me quite religious. It's not just inspiring (a much overused word), it's more a yardstick by which to measure, a feeling that sits inside of you and helps you to think.

I love Picasso, he's endlessly inventive and prolific, an extraordinary man and an extraordinary artist. I'm fascinated by the ceramics he decorated, his etchings, his drawings. Milton Avery and Richard Diebenkorn, two American colourist painters, appeal, as does Robert Kushner's textile/collage work. I also like what Mimmo Palladino does both in sculpture and in painting, it's so intense, so pared down, so moving. And I love the work of the Navajo Indians – it gives me tremendous excitement when I see it, especially in this strong south-western light.

I always have loved weave. My parents were Polish immigrants, and at home we were surrounded by rolled up kilims and carpets. When I trained in Poland I visited my relatives as well, and there the kilims are nailed up on the walls, they cover chairs and sofas. This familiarity with textiles formed part of my interest for a rather unusual medium.

Tapestry demands a huge investment of time and concentration. It's a gruelling, often frustrating, medium. It's huge physical demands force me to clarify my ideas, which for a very impulsive person is a good discipline. But I'm not obsessed by technique. Once it's there, there's no need to spend hours perfecting it. I let my warps wobble and I'm not embarrassed by it. Like painters who let the paint drips show. Getting the perfect tapestry doesn't interest me.

I don't compromise, I absolutely don't. I lost a commission when they wanted me to change things which I didn't feel I could. We parted without any animosity. I got my design fee and we parted quite amicably. It's got to look right and please me – that's my motto. Yes I want to please others, but I can't do that at my expense.

I certainly don't relate to translating David Hockneys into tapestry. I don't think making is a group activity. That's why, when other people make my work, they make it strictly to my rules. I'll define the shade, I'll mix the colours, define the texture, the yarns; I make my cartoons, I square them up. It's a very important part of the thinking onto tapestry. Having other people make my tapestries is determined by sheer practicality – the bigger the work, the harder it is to do it yourself – I mean what client would wait eighteen months until you've finished your tapestry? I'm generally called in at quite a late stage by the architect who wants something completed within just a few months.

I can't work with others in my studio – I've tried it and don't like it – it's too personal a space, I even feel threatened if my kids go in there. So I get it done to my rules, outside. I like the challenge of a public commission – who doesn't enjoy getting paid to do something you'd do anyway! The audience is there automatically – it's a terrific ego trip. I don't think its ever turned sour on me. Some commissioners can be very suspicious of contemporary art and imagery. But the process of working through the project with the artist changes them – and I find this conversion process very exciting.

What gets me here in LA is that everything is so new. You can be anyone here. Training, background, 'pedigree' count for so little. In England that would seem impossible – if you hadn't passed through a 'decent' art college you'd be lucky to be shown on Hyde Park railings. Here you're judged by what you produce, you're as good as the next person. It's so humbling for us Europeans.

Woven Tapestry (1988)
88" x 156", 225 x 400cm
(Commissioned for Fidelity Investments)

All this training and where are my colleagues from the RCA? I mean we all had a BA and postgraduate diplomas and this, that and the other, and now I think I'm the only one of my contemporaries still working – and I was by no means the most talented! I think it's scandalous, I really do. It's very tough in this field. The whole business is tough. It's to do with determination and luck and persistence. As in nature, your energy levels are so high when you're young. You take your biggest risks, you knock on doors, you sit up late and talk about ideas with people, you hitch to an opening in Edinburgh, you pawn your car to go to a Festival in Berlin. As you get older, your energy goes down, and unless you've been propelled early on into success, it's very tempting just to sit back and give up and do something else.

But once you're up there you'll carry on whatever the costs. I don't want people to think I'm totally euphoric – like everyone else I have my periods of self doubt, of being down. 'Why am I doing this, it's so hard to do, and such a hard world to do it in?'

But you do it because it's what you do, like you get dressed in the morning, like you eat, like you live with your partner. Without the commissions I'd still do it. You do it because that's what you do and you don't know any better. I'm pleased that ultimately I can leave something worthwhile behind me, and tapestry certainly has a history of longevity! There's something magical about the way a tapestry glows on the wall.

Ideas for Tapestry (1995–96)

Gouache and collaged paper

12" x 6", 30 x 15cm

Marta Rogoyska

Born

    1950, Beckenham, Kent

Education and Awards

    1971–73 – Leeds Polytechnic, BA (Hons) Fine Art

    1974–77 – Royal College of Art, MA Tapestry

    1975 – RCA, Travel Bursary

    1976 – Sanderson Scholarship, Aubusson, France

    1978 – British Council Scholarship, Warsaw Academy, Poland

    1979 – Crafts Council Grant

    1984 – British Council Travel Award, Germany

Ideas for Tapestry (1995–96)
Gouache and collaged paper
12" x 9", 30 x 23cm

Selected Exhibitions

    1988 – World Tapestry Today, Sydney

    1988 – British Council Craft, Toyko and Kyoto

    1989–90 – The Narrative Voice, Musée Lurçat, Aubusson (tour)

    1990 – Pentagram British Design Exhibition, Japan

    1992 – The New Academy Gallery, London

    1994 – HeimTextil, Frankfurt

    1995 – Woven Image, Contemporary British Tapestry, Barbican Centre (tour)

Selected Public Commissions

    Coca Cola, UK Headquarters

    The British Medical Association, London

    Fidelity Investments, Tunbridge Wells

    Sun Oil International Headquarters, London

    Withington Girl's School, Manchester

    The Brompton National Heart and Lung Association, London

    Trainload Freight, London

    Glaxo Headquarters, Stevenage

Collections

    V&A Museum, London

    Crafts Council of Great Britain

    The Whitworth Art Gallery, Manchester

    Museum of Modern Art, Tokyo

    Leeds City Art Gallery

    Castle Howard

The artist would like to acknowledge the assistance with weaving various tapestries of:
Joan Baxter, Dyllis Spinson, Leo Oliver and West Dean Tapestry Studios under Valerie Power.

There's definitely an affinity between the abstract, improvisational fabric of music and my work. If you like, these are spontaneous jazz improvisations in collage or tapestry.

Ideas for Tapestry (1995–96)
Gouache and collaged paper
10" x 5", 25 x 12cm

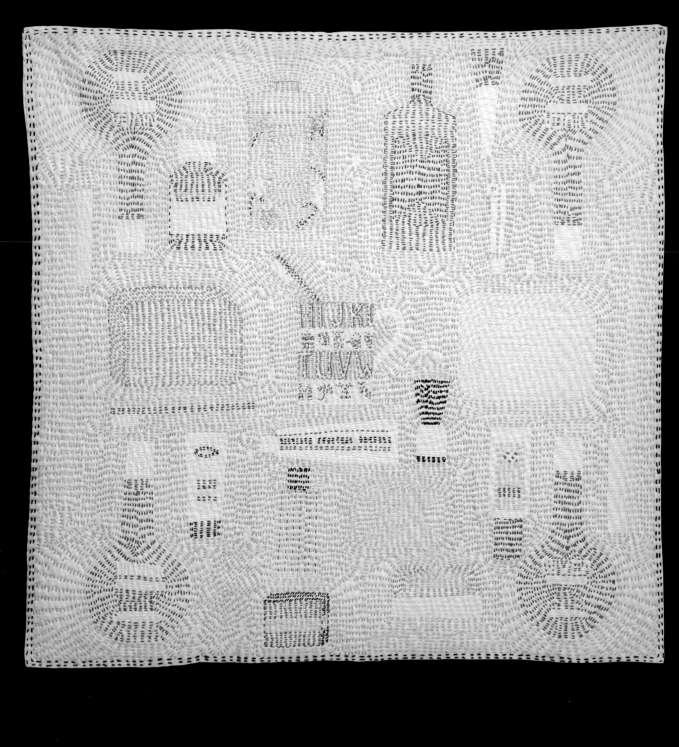

Lynn Setterington

In my work I'm making a subtle comment about possessions, some old and some new. They are portrayed as if in a diary, some affectionately, others slightly tongue-in-cheek.

Opposite: The Bathroom Shelf (1989)
Hand-embroidered quilt
23" x 23", 60 x 60cm

Detail

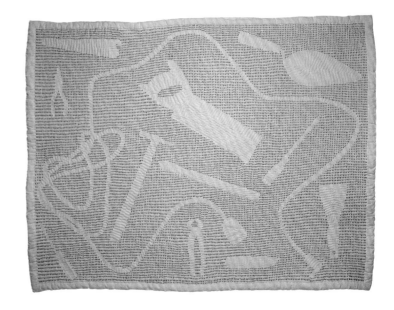

Home Alone (1995)
Hand-embroidered quilt
27" x 35", 70 x 90cm

My work is making a subtle comment about possessions, some old and some new.
They are portrayed as if in a diary, some affectionately, others slightly tongue-in-cheek.
I have a large collection of old kitchen utensils: tea-strainers, egg-whisks, potato-mashers
and the like, objects I keep around me at home. Some of them may find their way into a
piece. All the objects I choose to record are ones I'm familiar with, and usually fond of.
Some are becoming obsolete, we're losing the sense of what they were originally for.
With some I'm questioning whether we really need all these gadgets, with others,
the thoughts and memories they evoke.

A few years ago I worked part-time at the V & A Museum for six months in the textile
department. It was fascinating to see how the department operated. At the time they
were cataloguing their reserve collection onto computer, so we could inspect things that
not even the head of the department had seen, like The Legend of St Tristan, an Italian
quilt from the 1390s. I considered museum curating as a possible career for a while,
but decided against it as it would have meant giving up most of my own studio time.

I did a lot of tapestry weaving at college, and my own dyeing – I was very interested in
how colours work together – that interest remains but now it comes out in a more
subtle form in the embroideries. I think it's crucial as a practioner not to lose touch with
the materials, with the physicality of cloth and thread. If I were designing on paper,
and giving it to be stitched by someone else, something would be lacking.

My embroideries take so long that I generally work out the composition in advance –
I don't want to get half way through a piece and then feel unhappy with it. I'll do a series
of small-scale studies in my sketch book, some of which may then be taken further to a
large scale drawing. This would form the basis of a cartoon which I then transfer onto
the lightweight cotton.

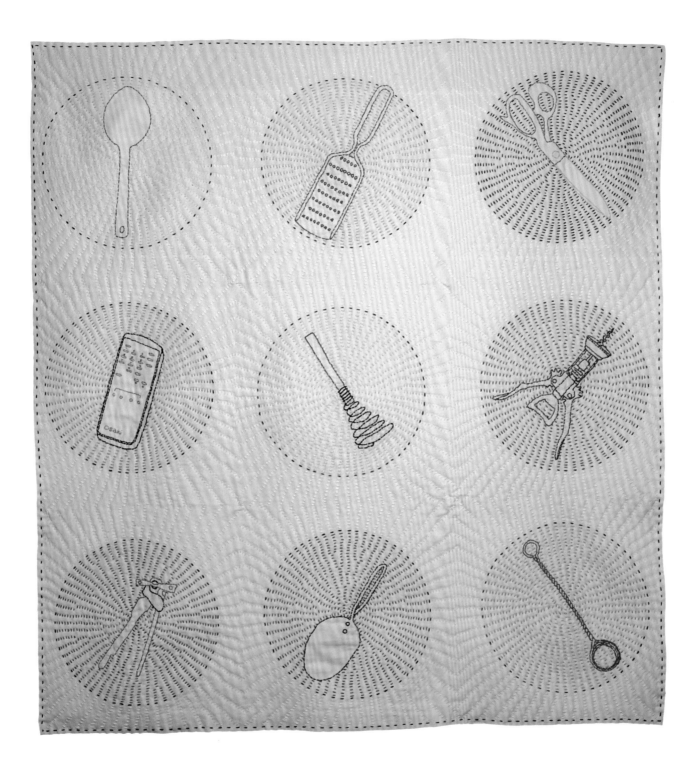

Remote Control (1996)
Hand-emboidered quilt
36" x 34", 93 x 88cm

The appearance of simplicity can be deceptive! Many people find the circular motif, creating a Catherine-wheel effect, almost impossible to stitch: it's all to do with the spacing of the stitches.

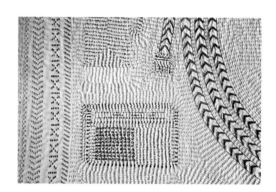

The top fabric is cotton sheet poplin or fine cotton lawn; the middle layer may be muslin or wadding, and the back cloth is a basic pillow cotton. The choice of the top fabric is important not only because a lot of it is visible; also because too stiff a cotton makes the stitching very difficult. I've been experimenting recently with yellow or green top fabrics – I've used mostly neutral coloured ones until now.

I hand-stitch all my work myself. I don't sew every day – for the sake of my fingers as well as my head. I don't use a thimble – I'd find it a hindrance. Instead I end up with sticking-plaster on my fingers. People say 'Your work must drive you mad!' And sometimes it does. But you can't get the quality of hand-stitching any other way. I could use a machine saddle-stitch – I've tried, but the stitching seems so regular and characterless – it doesn't have the individual, idiosyncratic quality I'm after.

I'm quite catholic in my tastes. I like world folk art, such as the naive wallpaintings I saw in India. I enjoyed an exhibition in Manchester of hand-painted signs from barbershops in Kenya; also 'Rites of Passage' at the Tate which had installations and sculpture. The exhibition which really changed how I work was the 'Woven Air' exhibition which I saw at the Whitechapel Art Gallery in London in 1988 where I saw kanthas for the first time. Kanthas are made by Bengali women – they're often made from old saris patched together – the softness of the fabric through years of wear makes them much easier to manipulate. They're embroidered with images of domestic objects: combs, lamps, nutcrackers, mirrors, and so on. Women also include images of things they'd like to acquire, such as umbrellas or earrings.

After seeing the exhibition I went home and started my own versions. I was excited with the results, and carried on working in that way for several months. In **Sowing Seed** the watering can and hose pipe relate to kanthas, which often have a lotus in the centre, representing regrowth or regeneration. At the time I shared a studio in Brixton with some painters and sculptors, I was very thrilled that Audrey Walker bought one of the new pieces at an open studio sale we held. It's always encouraging to get positive feedback after so much isolation in the studio.

This interest in kanthas has recently led me to travel to India, visiting around Rajasthan, Gujarat, and on to Bangladesh, with its wonderful hand-painted rickshaws, lush green landscape and rivers... the social, cultural and geographical setting that kantha embroidery grew up in. Making kanthas is one occupation women can do there without much opposition. It doesn't involve travelling too far from home, and, once trained, women can earn a 'reasonable' wage.

Sowing Seed (1992)
Hand-embroidery on white cotton sheet
59" x 50", 150 x 127cm

In India I visited the Crafts Museum in Delhi and the Calico Museum in Ahmedabad, both of which have wonderful collections of historical kanthas and sujnis (similar to a kantha but with larger stitches). There are very few sujnis and kanthas in British collections, so it was a real privilege to see so many at first-hand.

Kanthas look simple in their techniques. Made up of variations of running-stitch, it was this simplicity that initially appealed to me. But having tried some of the more complicated patterns, I discovered appearances can be deceptive! Many people find the circular motif, creating a Catherine-wheel effect, almost impossible to stitch: it's all to do with the spacing of the stitches.

My work moved on from the multi-coloured pieces to experimenting with single-coloured ones, particularly white on white. You can alter the surface of a cloth through the direction of the stitching, its size, and the spacing used. Very little hand-embroidery is done on a large scale nowadays, because of its time-consuming nature. The size of the kanthas I had seen encouraged me to try to work on a bigger scale.

DIY (1993)
Hand-embroidered quilt
26" x 27", 66 x 69cm
(Collection of Crafts Council of Great Britain)

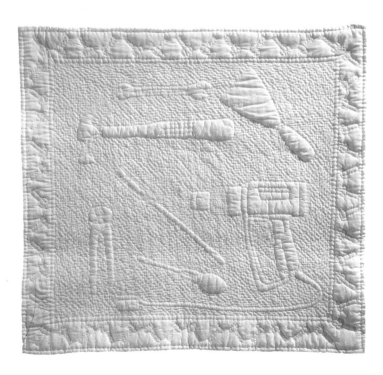

I liked the paradox of doing a pristine white piece about messy decorating! Traditional North Country quilts tend to include objects such as baskets of flowers. I depicted more confrontational images such as drill, hammer and paint stripper.

The Wormery (1996)
Appliqué and hand-embroidered quilt, cotton muslin,
found fabrics and cotton thread
9" x 11", 24 x 29cm

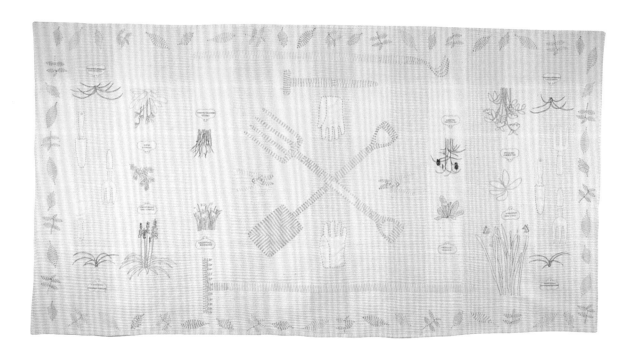

Unsung Heroes (1995)
Hand-embroidered quilt
59" x 121", 150 x 310cm
(Living at Belsay commission)

I also started to look at British quilts – whole cloth quilts as opposed to patchwork, traditionally made in the North East of England and in Wales. The challenge was how to make white on white visible. With the coloured quilts I had made previously, I could stitch the objects first, then bring the whole piece together through the use of background colour, which was crucial. Different colours could highlight shapes in different areas. With the white on white quilts, this wasn't possible. Instead, the problem was solved by raising the work, using a thicker wadding rather than just another layer of cloth. This helped to differentiate objects and to show them in relief.

The gardens of Belsay Hall were the starting point for **Unsung Heroes**, the quilt I was commissioned to make when I was Artist in Residence. The flowers I chose to portray were all early spring ones – though I didn't want to do just floral motifs. I also looked at a lot of garden tools and implements. Gardening is something that strikes a chord in me. I was brought up with. My dad taught rural science and was a keen gardener.

The piece also stemmed from the quilt traditions in the North East. As part of the Residency I visited small village schools, which were tiny – about 30 pupils in the school and, as part of the project, the children came in turn to work with me at the Hall. Their parents and grandparents had traditional quilts at home, either in use on their beds or else kept as heirlooms, to be passed on to the next generation. Technically speaking, the vertical stripes are a reference to strippy quilts, cloth made up of strips of left-over fabric from quilts. It's something particular to that area. I made the striped cloth from a yellow ground fabric, and stitched in the blue and yellow eight-inch stripes individually. It was the biggest piece I've ever done, and quite exhausting to make.

I don't consider myself to be a tidy person. I use my eye to measure things. The stitches aren't intended to be even or precise. Each stitch is an individual mark. I feel in control of my work. Maybe that's what others interpret as being neat.

Lynn Setterington

Born

1960, Doncaster

Education and Awards

1978–1979 – York College of Arts and Technology, Foundation Course

1979–1982 – Goldsmiths' College, London, BA (Hons) Textiles

1996 – Research trip to Bangladesh and India (funded by North West Arts and Manchester Metropolitan University)

Selected Exhibitions

1992 – Threadworks, Stitched Textiles Exhibition, Christchurch, New Zealand

1992 – Out of the Frame, Crafts Council Gallery, London (tour)

1994 – Darlington Arts Centre, Darlington

1994 – What is Embroidery? Whitworth Art Gallery, Manchester

1995 – Sampler Exhibition, Mobilia Gallery, Cambridge, MA, USA

1995 – Out of the Ordinary, Oldham Art Gallery (solo, tour)

1995 – Making Sense, Royal Albert Museum Exeter, Crafts Exhibition (tour)

1996 – William Morris: 'Reassessing the Legacy'.
   Whitworth Art Gallery, Manchester (tour)

Public Commissions

1993 – Darlington Arts Centre

1995 – Living at Belsay (English Heritage, Northern Arts and Northumberland
   County Council)

Collections

Crafts Council of Great Britain

Whitworth Art Gallery Manchester

Embroiderers' Guild, London

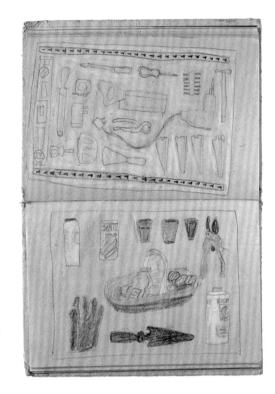

Sketch-book

The Back Gate (1996)
Etching and aquatint
6" x 5", 15 x 14cm

**Etchings have become important to me over the
last couple of years as a way of producing images
more quickly, getting out more ideas and working
on a different scale.**

Jo Barker

I see myself primarily as a designer/maker rather than a fine artist. But the image I create has such a painterly quality that it can easily cross over into the fine art world. I like the contradiction.

Lush Blue (1993)
Woven tapestry, mohair warp, wool, cotton, linen,
embroidery and metallic thread
47" x 48", 119 x 121cm

Opposite: detail

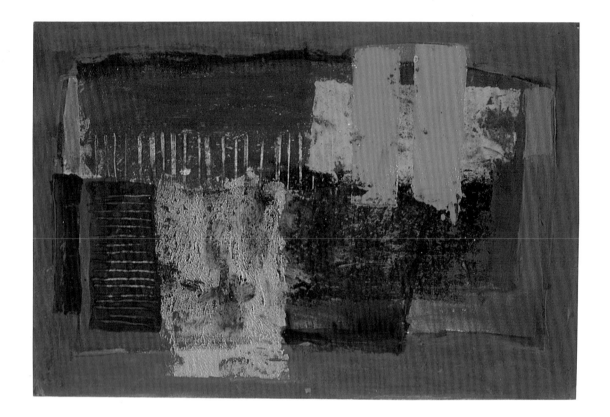

I like it when people gasp when they see my work. It's an emotional effect that I'm after, and not just a casual glance: I want the viewer to get drawn into the tapestry. I want there to be this sense of buzz and fizz, that makes your eye jump around.

Everyone has their natural, instinctive palette, and I'm happy to continue exploring mine: blues, greens, oranges and reds. Maybe one day I'll become cool and spare, but for the time being I'm absolutely fascinated by the intensity of colour once it is woven. Patrick Heron is someone I really admire, the way his work has gradually evolved through his working life. Colour has been a driving force for him too, as well as the inspiration of his surroundings in Cornwall.

Around the edge of **Ellipse** is a fine line of orange. I want this to play on the periphery of vision, so that the eye is drawn to the centre where the ellipse is spinning on the cooler background. Tapestry lends itself very well to this exploration. I love the luxury of the medium. It's very different from paint, because once a surface is made from wool and cotton, light is absorbed rather than reflected. And this creates a far more sumptuous quality.

I work on a high warp loom using the traditional Gobelin technique. The large tapestries are woven on black mohair warp, the miniatures on fine cotton warp. I like the quality of the mohair, it's a bit softer and creates a slightly more supple finish. I use black because traces of the mohair fibres emerge between the weaving, and intensify the colour.

Tapestry Design (1993)
Acrylic, oil bar
5" x 8", 13.5 x 20.5cm

It's quite subtle, but I like knowing it's there. I put a lot of time into blending the colours to soften the effect, creating the look of a spontaneous, painted brush-mark. Mixing tones and colours softens one shape into the next. Technically it's slow, but it does make it more interesting while I'm weaving.

People tell me I must be a very patient person to do what I do. But I actually think I'm quite the opposite. When I'm weaving I aim to do so much a day, and keep going until it's completed. Setting myself a daily target stops me from thinking 'Oh my God, there's so much to do'. In fact, the larger the tapestry, the more exciting it is to start.

When I work I'm surrounded by all the yarns, like a painter's palette. I'll spend a few weeks designing, regardless of whether it's for a commission or for exhibition work. When I'm designing, I work on small paintings, building up the space in layers, intuitively placing one colour next to another. Once the design is selected, paints, brushes, and sketchbooks all get put away, and out comes the wool; and I concentrate on weaving. My studio goes through several face lifts each year.

Sketch-book
Acrylic, oil bar, oil pastel

I studied a foundation course at Carlisle. It had a very broad syllabus with a strong emphasis on design. Lynne Curran taught me tapestry weaving – she appeared with large hanks of wools, stacks of slides, and suddenly this whole subject that I had never heard of opened up. I also enjoyed printed textiles and ceramics. In fact I was accepted by Manchester to study printed textiles. Looking back, I find it weird to think I might have gone down that path! But when I went to Edinburgh the print department said they felt my work was better suited to tapestry.

I've lived in Edinburgh now since 1982. It's not the tapestry connection I'm so conscious of so much as the cosmopolitan culture, the feeling of history in the city, and the fact that you can be out in the countryside very easily. I'll most likely stay put now.

Since 1990 I've been teaching part-time at Cumbria College of Art and Design on the HND Design/Crafts course. We work one-to-one with the students, covering areas like three-dimensional structure; experimental work with wire; exploration of the nature of fibre; and tapestry weaving in two and three dimensions. Recently I've been doing some teaching at Glasgow School of Art. Contact with the students is invigorating and challenging; but weaving is so exhausting that I try to keep my teaching down to one day a week.

Getting my first corporate commission was a real fluke. I was having some colour copies done at a local copy shop and I had my folder out on the counter, with the tag 'tapestry weaver' on it. In rushed an architect to pick up some prints – she saw the folder and said 'Oh great, just what we are looking for!' I didn't know what to expect, but eventually the client turned out to be Guinness the brewers. Once one client has given you their seal of approval it gives the next person confidence. One commission leads to another.

All my commissions have involved an art agency, consultant or architect. I've never really had any problems with the business side of the work, except that once I spent two months on designs for a corporate client who then decided that, due to the economic downturn, they wanted to drop the whole project – no design fee. I learned my lesson: get things confirmed in writing first. Maybe tapestry weavers are luckier than some – producing relatively few pieces each year means there's less time needed for paperwork.

Ideally I'd like to have one or two commissions a year with some exhibition work, and space to enjoy life as well. Last year's workload was too much. I was awful to live with, I know I was – hardly a weekend off. I realised I've got to manage my time more efficiently.

Ellipse (1994)
Woven tapestry
63" x 85", 160 x 216cm

Around the edge of Ellipse is a fine line of orange. I want this to play on the periphery of vision, so that the eye is drawn to the centre where the ellipse is spinning on the cooler background.

But you never know what's around the corner. I could employ other people to do all the weaving and just spend my time doing designs, but I enjoy the intimate experience of seeing a project right through to the end. If I have a really tight deadline I employ a friend, someone I know I can trust and work with; but most of the time I prefer to work alone.

I'm an intuitive, hands-on tapestry weaver. I'm constantly making decisions, that's what makes it interesting. At least you have a big physical result at the end of it. If I worked in a bank what would I have to show at the end of the day – nothing so tangible or rewarding perhaps. I do what I do because I enjoy it. You've got to know that this image in front of you can sustain you for weeks or months. The last thing you want is to be halfway through a tapestry and get bored with it, or feel that the design isn't working.

I see myself primarily as a designer/maker rather than a fine artist. But the image I create has such a painterly quality that it can easily cross over into the fine art world. I like the contradiction.

Purple Border (1990)
Woven tapestry
54" x 48", 137 x 122cm

Lightning (1995)
Woven tapestry
44" x 42", 112 x 108 cm
(One of a series of four commissioned by City University, London)

Jo Barker

Born
    1963, Ulverston, Cumbria

Education and Awards
    1981–82 – Cumbria College of Art and Design, Foundation Year
    1982–85 – Edinburgh College of Art, BA (Hons) Design:
        Tapestry with Printmaking (First Class)
    1985–86 – Edinburgh College of Art, Post Graduate Diploma (Commended)
    1985 – Edinburgh College of Art, Andrew Grant Postgraduate Scholarship
    1988 – Scottish Development Agency, Aberdeen City Art Gallery
        and Museums, Residency
    1994 – Scottish Arts Council, Artistic Development Award

Selected Exhibitions
    1990 – Jo Barker and Friends, Aberdeen City Art Gallery and Museums
    1993 – Interwoven II, Smith's Galleries, London
    1995 – British Tapestry, Harley Gallery, Notts.
    1995 – Raw Materials, Scottish Contemporary Textiles (tour)
    1996 – Fibre Art, Brewery Arts Centre, Cumbria
    1996 – Woven Image, Contemporary British Tapestry, Barbican Centre (tour)

Selected Public Commissions
    1990–91 – Guinness Head Office, Edinburgh
    1992 – Bank of China, London
    1993 – Cable & Wireless, Coventry (rug made in collaboration with
        Edinburgh Tapestry Company)
    1995 – City University, Centenary Building, London
    1995–96 – Scottish Office, Victoria Quay, Edinburgh

Collections
    Princess Anne: gift from Edinburgh College of Art
    Aberdeen City Art Gallery and Museums

Ellipse II (1996)
Woven tapestry
10" x 15", 26 x 40 cm

Scottish Office Tapestry, Edinburgh (1996)
96" x 195", 244 x 496cm

Detail

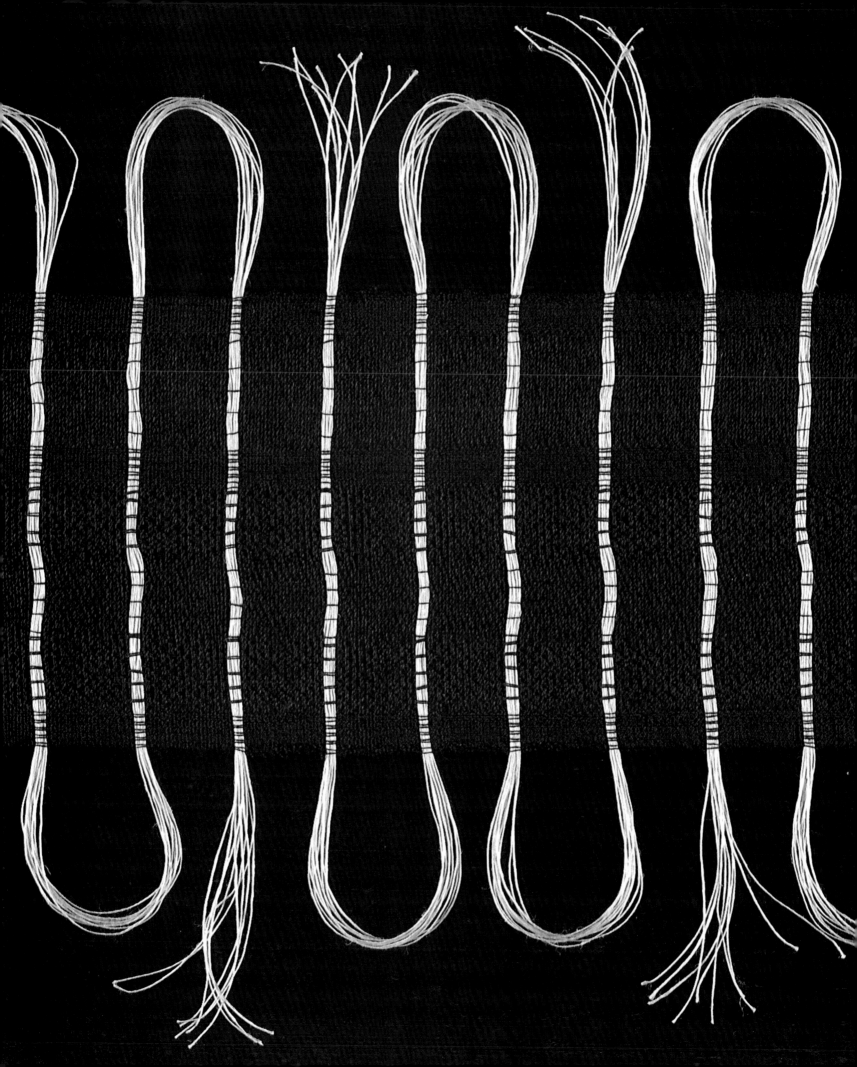

Greg Parsons

I'm a perfectionist by nature. But you need to make mistakes, you need to let go and try out new colours, a bizarre yarn... You need to discover the undiscovered, otherwise you just find out what already exists.

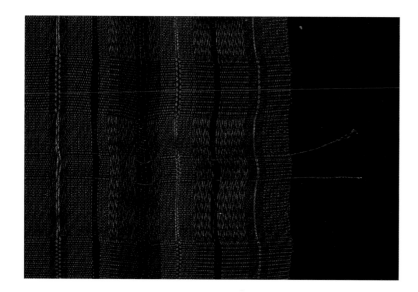

Rubicon – Pink 1 (detail) (1994)
Woven textile, mercerised cotton, textured polyester,
coated copper wire
7" x 56", 16 x 142cm

Opposite: Sidewinder (1994)
Woven piece, mercerised cotton linen
3" x 45", 8 x 114cm

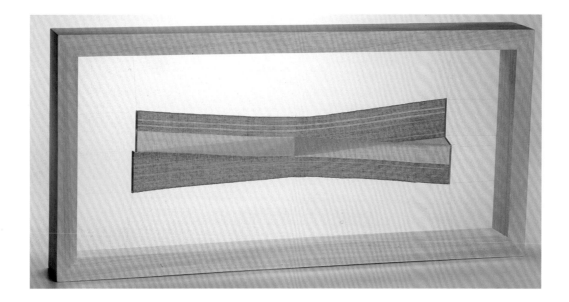

Kites were my first departure into one-off framed pieces. The initial idea came from box kites and stunt kites. Most work I'd done until then had been around ten inches square. I wanted to make these much smaller, and I wanted them displayed as three-dimensional objects. This was resolved by displaying them in a boxed frame. Finishing them off with fine silver gave them a very precious, jewel-like quality.

Following on from the Kites, I started considering a different colour palette, taking contemporary Japanese architecture as my starting point with it's wonderful shades of grey and steel. I began to introduce metal into my woven structures. I find metallic colours just as beautiful as intense, bright ones – they have a real sophistication.

I began to think about how architecture is layered, with glass and steel, its internal structure; and I started introducing nylon monofilament which gave the fabric transparent characteristics. Architecture and weave have a lot in common, both are built of lines, horizontals and verticals. It's an ideal relationship.

Now I'm finding colours from nature which I've somehow avoided in the past. I'm looking at organic sources, at the work of certain environmental artists. Andy Goldsworthy would for example isolate the red leaves from a maple tree, and cover a rock with them, so that the rock takes on a whole new identity. It could be an artificial effect, but in fact it's very natural. He's creating interesting juxtapositions of colour and texture within the natural environment, in the same way that I'm attempting to create a new setting in our interior environment.

At Derby I was starting to think about fabrics both in terms of layering and movement. Towards the end of the course I began to consider directing the fabrics towards the fine art field. When I was Artist in Residence at Ruthin in Wales I developed this further. Rather disappointingly the most common reaction to the work in my open studio was 'What are they for?' Many people still have difficulty interpreting textiles as pieces of art in their own right. I'm not satisfied with just one category. I wasn't sure that was the direction I wanted to pursue indefinitely. One area feeds another.

Diversions Four (1995)
Woven triple-cloth, mercerised cotton and fine silver
16" x 4", 41 x 10cm

Kites (from a series of 14) (1994)
Woven triple-cloth, mercerised cotton and fine silver
4" x 4", 10 x 10cm

The reason I've come as a postgraduate to the Royal College of Art was to find new things. I'm currently doing some work on the power Jacquard loom. The beauty of it is that once you've got the design you can produce a quantity of fabric quickly. Traditionally the Jacquard loom would be used for decorative work, but I want to use it more structurally, to explore how I can make a layered fabric in a different way.

The **Sample** has a movement to it. It's a conventional double cloth, but linked, in a fragile way. On the loom it was very formal, with regular sections of the top orange cloth taken down and joined to the bottom red cloth, and then the warp taken back up to the surface. As it came off the loom it looked much freer and more organic: the slash-like spaces move, the two cloths shift from side to side as you handle them. I'm interested in that movement. I think it's got very exciting prospects on a large scale. On a blind for example, there is some natural movement, the breeze blows them, you touch them, you get different perspectives on the fabric.

I'm also investigating different fibres – synthetics in particular. Until recently I'd concentrated on cotton, with nylon and fine wires, but there are so many new things available, so many types of nylons and polyesters. Currently, fabric designers are mixing fibres: Lycra for example is becoming finer and finer and is being used with cotton and wool, giving added elasticity and strength.

I want to do some work for the interiors' market, designing fabrics for power loom production that have commercial potential. I also want to investigate the possibilities of initial ideas and structures I've tried on the hand loom, developing them for use in blinds and drapes. I want to investigate upholstery fabrics as well, possibly working with a furniture student, which I think would be very exciting. I see my interior settings being something very different, maybe three-dimensional. I've already explored double and triple cloths and I want to take this further.

Sample (1996)
Woven double-cloth, mercerised cotton, nylon crystal, viscose, tinned copper wire
7" x 8", 17 x 20cm

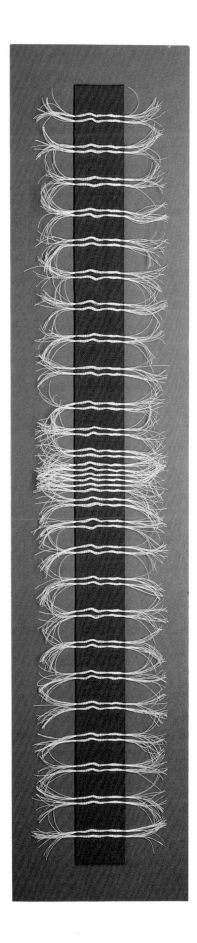

Organised Chaos II (1995)

Woven piece, mercerised cotton, linen

44" x 8"; 110 x 19cm

Organised Chaos deals with organisation, repetition and control, but also breaks from that restraint – the linen threads have a mind of their own.

Kites (from a series of 14) (1994)
Woven triple-cloth, mercerised cotton and fine silver
4" x 4", 10 x 10 cm

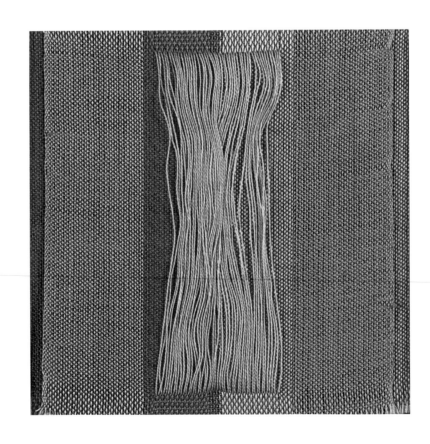

I also want to explore concepts in recent pieces much further, for example how the **Neck Piece** (which was inspired by the Lloyds building in London) could work on a larger, three-dimensional scale. It might entail looking at lighting and thinking about form. The emphasis will be on interior settings, and I'll be trying to escape preconceived notions of what curtain or upholstery fabric should look like, I'll be looking for something more challenging.

Inspiration filters through from many different sources. Sometimes there are so many ideas floating around, it's difficult to fix on one thing: that's when you need to just let go and play.

Mark Rothko's work is very abstract, his use of colour is amazing, not only a bright palette but also deep and quite intense. I've been interested in his work for some time, so it's filtered through: his more brightly coloured works for example, using very intense reds, yellows and oranges. I can see a relationship with the painter mixing together his paints on the palette, and the weaver interlacing threads to create a third colour. I can relate his work and ideas to my own abstraction.

I find objects, product design, architecture and fine art appealing. In textiles, I very much liked Lesley Mitchison's show 'A Scrutiny of Constraint', and the work of Sara Brennan, whose abstract forms remind me of Ben Nicholson.

I'm a perfectionist by nature, which can be a problem – sometimes I think about things too much without trying them out. You need to make mistakes; you need to let go and try out new colours, a bizarre yarn... You need to discover the undiscovered, otherwise you just find out what already exists.

Greg Parsons

Born

1970

Education and Awards

1989–90 Exeter Faculty of Art and Design, Foundation Course

1990–93 The University of Derby, BA (Hons) Textile Design – Weave (First Class)

1995–97 The Royal College of Art, London, MA Constructed Textiles – Weave

Selected Exhibitions

1991, 92 – Fabrex, Earls Court, London

1993, 94 – HeimTextil, Frankfurt

1993 – A Midsummer Night's Dream, The Gallery, The Ruthin Craft Centre,
North Wales

1993 – Texprint '93 – Interstoff, Frankfurt

1995–97 – A Contemporary Voice, Ruthin Craft Centre (solo, tour)

1995 – Crafts Council Foyer Showcase

1995 – Cedars of Lebanon, The Pump House,
Battersea, London

1996 – The Livingstone Studio, Hampstead, London

Neck Piece (1995)

Woven double-cloth, mercerised cotton, Lycra, linen, fine copper wire

7", 18cms approximate diameter

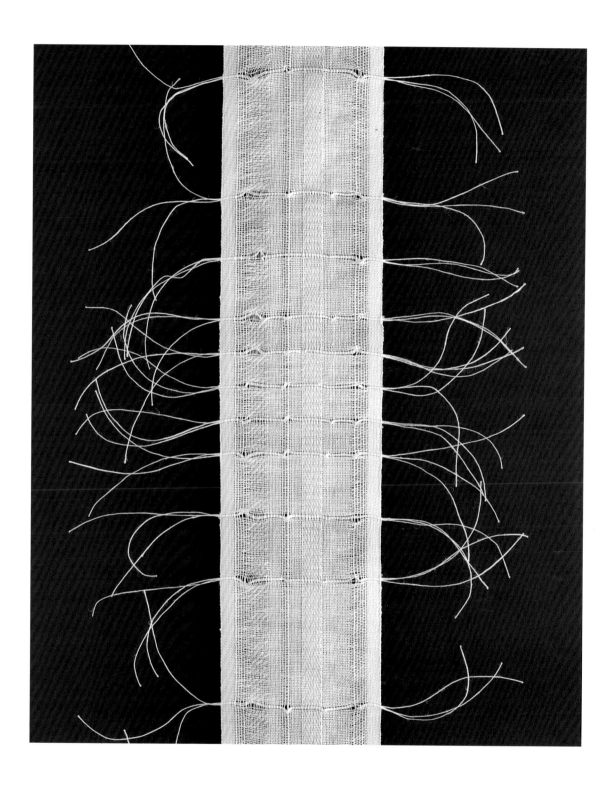

Metallic Elements (detail) (1994)
Woven piece, mercerised cotton, metallis, linen
3" x 18", 7 x 45cm

Jeanette Appleton

I'm not afraid to express unease in my work. After all, art should come from the soul, and which of us is totally settled?... Felt is an unpredictable medium. It shifts in the making.

Opposite: Ishtar Images (detail) (1994)
Dyed merino wool, printed silk organdie, stitch
68" x 17", 170 x 43cm

Past Shadows, Men-En-Tol (1994)
Dyed merino wool, printed silk organdie, stitch
57" x 87", 145 x 225cm

This triptych was influenced by a visit to the Pergamon Museum in Berlin where I walked through a temple to the Babylonian goddess Ishtar. The walls were covered with ceramic tiles depicting these strange mythical beasts.

It's interesting that a lot of fine artists use fibre in their work, people like Claes Oldenburg, who questions the authenticity and worth of the commodity; or Robert Morris. He would cut into industrial felt, and the shapes evolved from the way the material fell. There's not the intervention of a maker involved. The pieces are made by the essence of the material, it's as if they made themselves.

There is a lot of excellent work being made in felt world-wide, by people like Gunilla Sjöberg of Finland or Karen Page in America; and an active network of international feltmakers which I very much value. I believe that the world's political and religious boundaries are broken down wherever individual human contact is made. I have had a lot more opportunities to travel since I started working in felt, and this is enriching both in terms of visual stimuli and in terms of friendships. I try to keep an open mind, I try to find the common ground that lies between fine art and textile art; appreciating what both sides have to offer and constantly questioning myself about where I stand.

The wool in my work is not just about making textiles, but explores issues of possessions and personal space. I think our identity is often defined by what we choose to surround ourselves with. Many people seem restricted by their house or their possessions. I think I'm fortunate to rent my home – I've lived here overlooking these fields for twenty years now. I'm also fortunate in that I'll soon be travelling around the world. I'm going to Japan, Australia and Mongolia, where I'll be living in a yurt – an open, wooden structure covered by felt.

I first learnt about yurts when I was exploring ideas of containment and looking into primitive structures. Matisse writes about 'the metaphysics of doors and windows as gateways to a universe with no inside or outside, where inside always includes outside'. Mongolian yurts are made entirely of materials from the landscape: the hair of sheep, horses and camels. The nomads don't consider that they own the land – they borrow it. When it's time to move on they just roll up their yurt and carry it on their horses. Staying in a yurt, I'll be returning to the very beginning of my source.

Territorial Fossil Form 1 (1995)
Dyed merino wool, printed silk organdie, stitch
10" x 14", 26 x 36cm

Opposite: Ishtar Images, Triptych (detail) (1994)
Dyed merino wool, printed silk organdie, stitch
68" x 17", 170 x 43cm

The process starts off with pure merino wool. I dye it myself – a preoccupation with colour is present right from the outset. Different coloured wools are carded, pulled apart and layered, for example blue on red. Then the layers are rubbed together with hot soapy water poured on. This flattens the surface, causing the natural scales of the wool to bond. As the surface shrinks, the colours from the lower layers rise to the surface. So the exact colour blend is spontaneous and organic, and very difficult to control.

With other mediums you're mixing the colour palette before you apply the colours to the textile surface. With felt, you're mixing the colours as you build up the fibres. Felt has a will of its own, it has its own way of settling, you have to adapt to the unexpected shapes you're presented with.

When I come to sew, there's a choice whether to overlap the image or stitch the spaces around it. The nature of the felt making distorts a detailed shape, while the stitching redefines the character of a form. The beauty of it is that you're drawing and making the fabric at the same time.

Quite often I do separate pieces and collage them together with a stitched line. This stitched line, whether on the surface or hidden on the reverse, is the equivalent of a tonal drawn line in the composition. What I like about the stitching is it embosses the felt surface, rather like the scratching on the paper pieces. I use both hand and machine-stitch. I've found that a lot of preliminary drawing and research is needed. It gives me a source of imagery to work from; and the freedom to draw on the piece. It's given me the flexibility that allows the image to emerge out of the felt, rather than feeling I have to impose on it.

Fossilised Boundaries (1995)
Dyed merino wool, printed silk organdie, stitch
50" x 76", 128 x 194cm

Discovering the buried past through fragments of early Nordic settlements and vessels – an aerial view of a landscape in Denmark.

Papermaking, which I did for about five years, became a good in between stage from the drawing into the textile. **Bryce Canyon Myth** was inspired by the journey I made in 1991 from the Painted Valley in the USA to the Bryce Canyon.

The piece is made of hand-made paper, torn up, pulped down, then dyed repeatedly in layers. The surface is then embossed, marked with pencils and pastels, distressed, scratched.

The composition is taken from an accumulation of drawn shapes from my sketchbook, including shapes of the canyons and the never-ending horizon. Back home, further research into North American Indian mythology highlighted shapes I remembered seeing in the landscape, like the steps and the curve in the top part of the paper piece – these looked like a traditional form called a 'Mother Earth Vessel'. There was a Monet exhibition on at the Royal Academy when I got back that further heightened my perception of colour in landscape.

I worked with stronger, more intense colour after that trip than ever before. My daughter Zoe came with me, it was good to share the experience with her. There's a legend that the Coyote turned bad Indians into rocks – and two figures started appearing in the work; as if they had emerged from the rock formations. They seemed to be about us – Zoe was eighteen and becoming independent, it was like letting go of a part of motherhood. She'd been part of my space for so long. It was made more poignant letting go in that landscape with so much space.

Felt opens up a very direct and intimate path to an individual's creative sources. As soon as you handle the fleece and layer the colours, you're making a personal statement. Right from the starting point, it takes on the characteristics of the person handling it. There aren't too many interruptions or specific technical problems in the way of being creative with the material. And so felt is useful for people searching for their own identity.

Fossiled Territory I (1995)
Dyed merino wool, printed silk organdie, stitch
20" x 13", 50 x 32cm

Opposite: Bryce Canyon Myth (1991)
Hand-made paper, dyes, pastel, pencil
22" x 33", 57 x 84cm

Bryce Canyon Myth (detail) (1991)

Jeanette Appleton

Born

1949, Ongar, Essex

Education and Awards

1987–89 – Goldsmiths' College, Post-Graduate Diploma, Textile Art
(Commended)

1994–98 – Middlesex University, BA (Hons) Fine Art (in progress)

1989 – Hertfordshire Open Art Exhibition, joint First Prize (Textiles)

1993 – Hertfordshire Open Art Exhibition, First Prize (Textiles)

Selected Exhibitions

1990 – Chelsea Comes to California, Festival of Britain

1991 – Two-Person Show, Faith Nightingale Gallery, San Diego

1992 – Musee du Feutre, Mouzon, France

1992 – Maltings Art Centre, St Albans (solo)

1993 – Felt Works, Bankfield Museum, Halifax

1994 – The Sea, The Sea, New Fibre Art Show, University of Plymouth

1994 – Invited Exhibition of International Feltmakers, Hartbury, Gloucestershire

1995 – International Feltmakers Association, Mouzon, France

1995 – 3-Person show, CCA Galleries, Cambridge

1995 – Felt Directions, Collins Gallery, University of Strathclyde

1996 – European Textile Network Conference, '62 Group Exhibition,
Quarry Bank Mill, Styal, Cheshire

Collections

Sandra Lummis Fine Art Collection, London

Hertfordshire County Art Collection

KPMG Peat Marwick Ltd

Sketchbook
Pastel, pencil and dyes

Opposite: Fossiled Landscape II (1995)
Dyed merino wool, printed silk organdie, stitch
10" x 14", 26 x 36cm

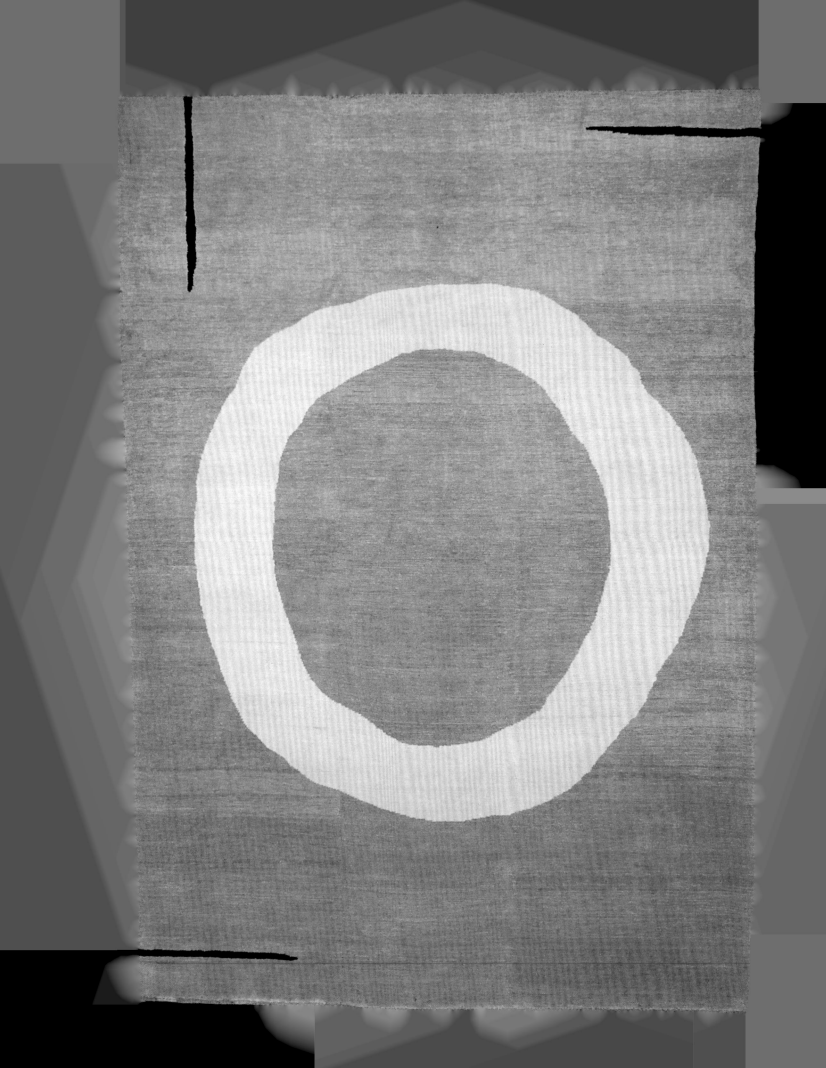

Kate Blee

The quality I want for a textile is for it to look like it's always been that way. I don't want you to be able to imagine it differently. We're all looking for undesigned design, to give birth to something that looks as though it's existed for ever.

Two Runners (1994)
Hand dyed and knotted wool
108" x 29", 275 x 75cm
(Limited edition for Christopher Farr)

Opposite: Rug (1994)
Hand dyed and knotted wool
71" x 96", 180 x 245cm
(Limited edition for Christopher Farr)

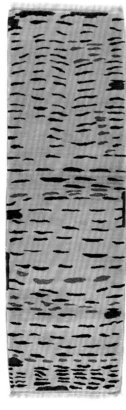 

The quality I want for a textile is for it to look like it's always been that way. I don't want you to be able to imagine it differently. We're all looking for undesigned design, to give birth to something that looks as though it's existed for ever.

It is very rare for me to look at a piece and be completely satisfied. But the rug I designed in 1992 (opposite) for a joint project with Christopher Farr still satisfies me today. The design, square rather than the more usual rectangular format, is balanced all round and allows approaching from each side. Leaving the black lines in was dangerous. They could have looked like outlines, but they hold in the colour and also add a playful quality to the structure. I like to set up a certain type of formality and then break through it, relax it, give it a human hand.

The pair of runners (page 103) which I designed two years later are modern interpretations of the basic principles of rug design. The right hand runner is traditional in terms of having a border around a field, but the border has been reduced to a series of dashes running off the edges. The long sides of the left hand runner are flecked every so often by red streaks to mark the edge. I wanted this piece to have a feeling of freedom and landscape, but to hold itself within the area of the rug.

My most recent design (page 102), is probably the simplest. I was aiming for strength and simplicity, something bold and serene. I wanted to pare away the design and see how little I could get away with.

Earlier on in the project I didn't trust this natural movement within the colour, so I would put in more detail. But in this piece I trust it. With just three lines I'm telling you 'This is the border of the carpet'. It was important that the circle shouldn't be symmetrical. I wanted it to have a human or natural mark-making quality.

All the yarn is dyed by hand so it is uneven. Where the rugs are knotted, tonal changes occur in the yarn, so there's no boredom, no uniformity. Instead you have a very natural movement of subtle tonal changes, they're not artificially 'designed-in'.

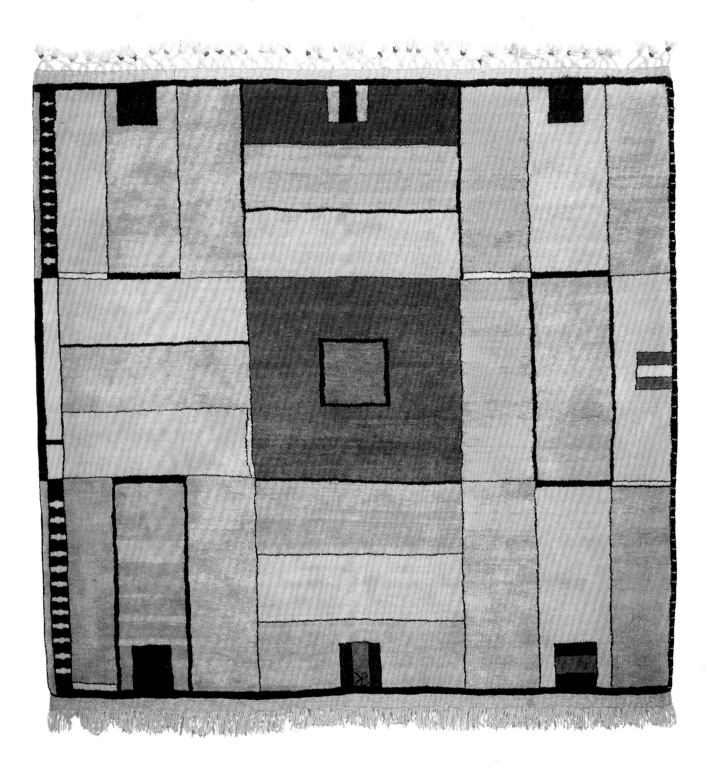

Rug (1992)
Hand-dyed and knotted wool
75" x 70", 191 x 178cm
(Limited edition for Christopher Farr)

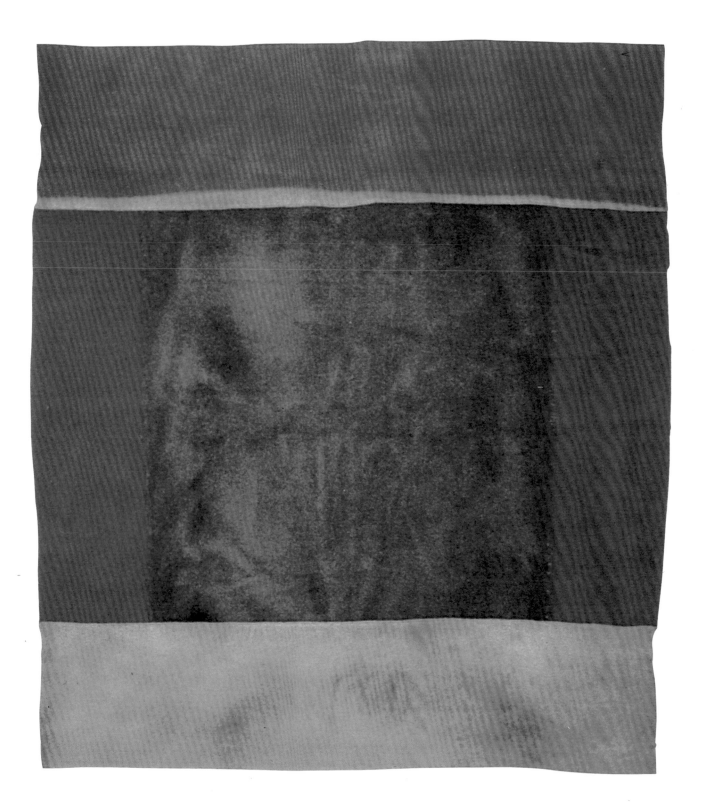

Sketch-book

Opposite: Wall Piece (1991)
Painted with acid dyes onto wool
23" x 16", 60 x 40cm

The selection of fabric has become an important part of the process. In the same way that in my sketch book I tend to use thick watercolour paper, because of the way it absorbs the paint, so my design will be influenced by the way in which the dye is absorbed by the cloth. When you're printing it's quite different, you can impose any image you want. But using the brush is a very organic thing, and the contact the brush makes with the cloth determines what kind of work you're going to get.

In woven textiles, fabric is constructed; but in paint and print there can be a superficial element to the piece where the dye only decorates the surface. I want to see the dye totally absorbed, for the colour to become a true part of the yarn, of the structure.

Mark Rothko has had the biggest impact on my work and will probably continue to do so. At college I saw his work, looked at how colour vibrated – he gave me the confidence to believe that colour was an issue in its own right. When I look at a building I'm looking at render colour next to brick, next to a shutter with peeling paint – texture and colours sitting next to each other. When I went to India, I was looking at the skin tone of the people next to the colour they wore, I wasn't looking at the patterns of their saris, I was looking at brownness next to redness.

Quite often sketches will be done when I'm travelling. They're not done so much to work from in the studio, but as something in their own right. It's very rare that something from the sketch book will end up on the cloth. The dyes I use are not catalogued. They are laid down, and then I see if it's the result I want. At college I used to adhere to dye recipes very strictly and make detailed notes, but if I went into all that now I'd never get anything done! I mix colour to full strength and then inter-mix those. I never attempt to repeat the colour.

One side of my work is putting the brush to fabric, but if my design ideas were limited to what I can produce in the studio, I'd be very frustrated: I never feel that there is enough time. You're only part way there when you've completed the cloth. Then it needs to go a further distance to find its purpose. It's mobile and flexible. I like that state of flux. With most of my painted pieces I would feel just as happy to have them hung on a wall as slung over a sofa, pulled around a body or crumpled up in the corner of a room. The market place demands that you determine the use so that it can be understood, but I enjoy the undefined nature and try to hang onto that.

In the world of textiles we're designers as well as artists. Opportunities arise in the commercial world that are very exciting – it's a world I'm happy to move into, that's challenging in its own right. I like my work to be used in a variety of ways.Sparking out in all directions is what gives me energy, and that's the way I'm going forward.

I want the colour to be so rich in itself that you could fall into it, or eat it, or pick it up. So three-dimensional that it vibrates. That is why my work has become simpler – I want people to say 'I love that colour'. The **Wall Pieces** are worked on a thick wool blanket. It's woven wool with a raised surface, so that it looks like felt, and absorbs vast quantities of dye. Although it was difficult to work, and infuriatingly slow to dry, it gave me the resonance I was looking for.

As a student at Edinburgh College of Art I was able to do a lot of work on cloth. In most colleges you'd have to book your time on the print table; but there were very few in my year, and the college was open 24-hours a day. So I came out with a good knowledge of working directly on cloth.

In every batch of work you do, one or two pieces should be outstanding. It's not that you get better and better, although with experience the decision making should get quicker. But you don't get enough of these pieces to make you so confident. You have to be restless. The more I go on with my work, the options for giving up get less and less! There are stages in my life where I'd have been quite prepared to give it all up, but the work has become more and more a part of me. I like my work, but I never like it enough to think it can't be improved next time round. There always seems to be so much more to discover. That's what keeps me going.

Scarf (1996)
Double crêpe de chine
41" x 17", 105 x 45cm

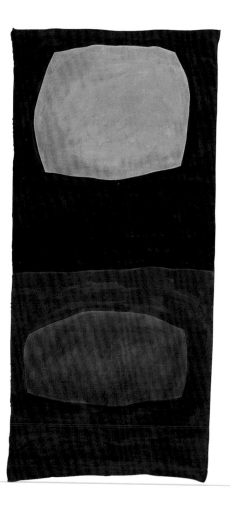

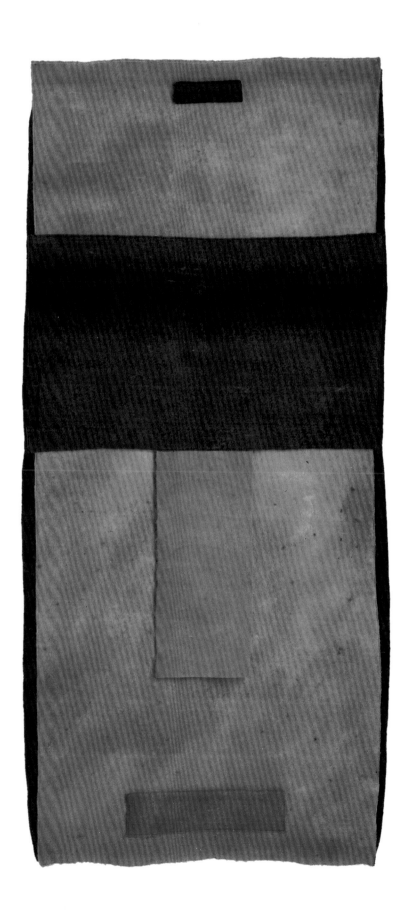

Wall Piece (1991)
Painted with acid dyes onto wool
67" x 24", 170 x 60cm

I want the colour to be so rich in itself that you could fall into it, or eat it, or pick it up. I want people to say 'I love that colour'.

Kate Blee

Born
    1961, London

Education and Awards
    1979–83 – Edinburgh College of Art, BA (Hons) (First Class)
    1983–84 – Edinburgh College of Art, Postgraduate Diploma in Design
    1983 – Andrew Grant Travel Scholarship, India, Clarion Bursary Award
    1985 – Crafts Council Setting Up Grant
    1986 – EDU Grant for Small Businesses

Selected Exhibitions
    1991 – Brave New Rugs, Royal College of Art, London
    1992 – Decorative Arts Today, Bonhams, London
    1992, 93 – Brave New Rugs 2, Christopher Farr
    1993 – Floor Show, Royal College of Art, London
    1994 – The Colour Blue, Vene Bunker
    1994 – Colour into Cloth, Crafts Council
    1995 – Rumble in the Jungle, South Bank Centre
    1995 – Clothes to Collect, Contemporary Applied Arts
    1996 – The Charleston Trust, Sussex
    1996 – Egg, Knightsbridge (solo)

Public Commissions
    1985, 87 – Two Altar Cloths, St Giles Cathedral, Edinburgh
    1992 – Series of Rugs, East Sussex National Golf Club
    1994 – Rug, Powergen

Selected Clients
    Design work: Habitat, Christopher Farr, Paul Smith, French Connection,
        Christine Foley Knitwear
    Graphics/Illustration: Citibank, Friends of the Earth, Paul Hamlyn Foundation

Collections
    Crafts Council of Great Britain
    Contemporary Arts Society

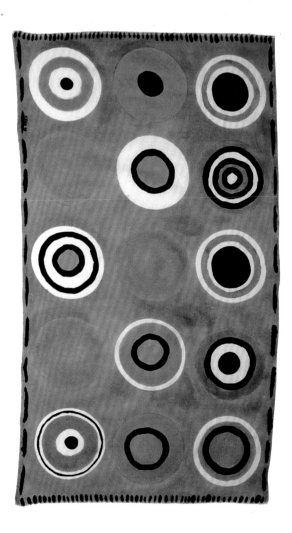

Shawl (1993)
Painted with acid dyes onto wool crêpe
78"x 39", 200 x100cm

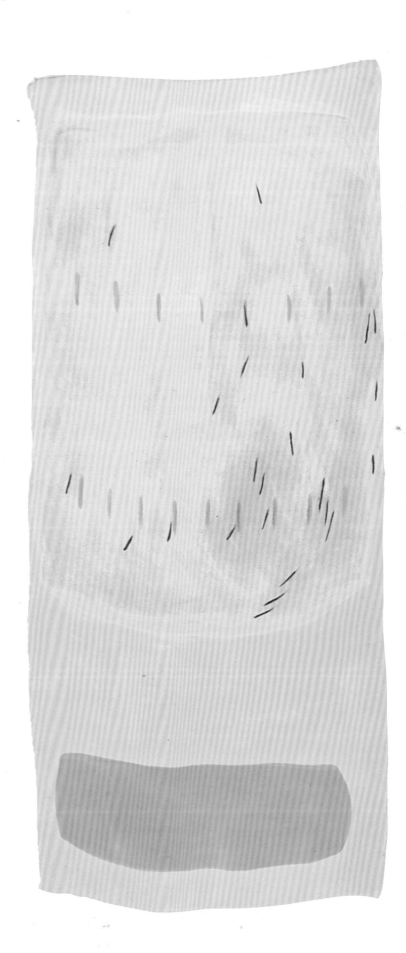

Scarf (1996)
Double crêpe de chine
41" x 17", 105 x 45cm

Cloth is a very strange thing. You're working most of the time on a two dimensional level, but the moment you pick it up it is a sculptural, mobile shape, and that's the notion I want resonating in the work.

Forthcoming titles:

Art Textiles of the World: Australia
ISBN 0 9526267 0 5

Art Textiles of the World: USA
ISBN 0 9526267 1 3

Art Textiles of the World: Japan
ISBN 0 9526267 4 8

Telos books are available from:

Telos Art Publishing
PO Box 125
Winchester SO23 7UJ
Great Britain
Fax +44 (0)1962 864727

Arcade Book Shop (Mail Order)
6 Fryern Arcade, Chandlers Ford,
Hampshire SO53 2DP
Telephone 01703 252083

Contemporary Applied Arts
London W1
Telephone 0171 436 2344

Crafts Council
London N1
Telephone 0171 278 7700

Also from a growing number of specialist international outlets:

America
Wellspring Gallery
Los Angeles
Telephone 310 441 4204
Fax 310 470 6424

Australia
Artisan Books
Melbourne
Telephone 03 9329 6042
Fax 03 9326 7054

Mill Hill Books
PO Box 80 Maleny
Telephone 074 942 081

Holland
Boekhandel van de moosdijk bv
Telephone 0493 496370
Fax 0493 493 549

Israel
Rubin Mass Ltd
POB 990 Jerusalem 91009
Telephone 972 2 277863
Fax 972 2 277 864

Sweden
Goteborgs
Box 25 117
S400 31 Goteborg
Fax 46 31 20 44 11